£500 and a bott

waiting to be claimed

Each copy of the Hertfordshire Restau ... a unique
number. One lucky number, chosen at ...]ue and a
bottle of champagne.

To find out if you have won, simply complete and return the form below or send a stamped self-addressed envelope with your name and address to the publishers of the Guide. No purchase is required and only one entry is allowed per person. You will be notified within fourteen days if you are the lucky winner. Terms and conditions overleaf. Good luck!

Everyone's a winner

This is one occasion where it really is the taking part that counts. Every reader who returns the form below will receive a free subscription to our four-monthly FOOD FOR THOUGHT newsletter.

FOOD FOR THOUGHT is a great way to keep up-to-date on the best places to eat out in Hertfordshire with essential news on new restaurants, new and changing menus, award winning restaurants together with news of local events and entertainment.

Lucky Number 02923

Name   Mr / Mrs / Miss / Ms / Other _____

Address   _____

            _____ Postcode _____

If you do NOT wish to receive your free copies of FOOD FOR THOUGHT, please tick this box ☐.
We may contact you from time to time to provide you with information about other publications produced by The Glove Box Guide Publishing Company. Your details will not be disclosed to any third party. If you do NOT wish to receive this information please tick this box ☐.

To assist with our market research, please answer the following questions:

1 Where did you buy this Guide or did you receive it as a present? _____

2 How did you hear about the Guide? _____

3 How many times do you eat out in a month?   1   2   4   10   20

4 Which is your favourite type of food? _____

5 How much do you pay, on average, per person each time you eat out? _____

6 Which is your favourite restaurant? _____

Thank you for your time and good luck with your 'Lucky Number' entry.

Terms and conditions

1 The winner will be notified within fourteen days of receipt of entry.

2 The winning number was randomly allocated before the Guide was printed.

3 The prize must be claimed no later than 31st July 2005.

4 If the prize is not claimed by the above date, the £500 prize money will be donated to a local charity, to be chosen by the publishers.

5 The £500 prize will be paid in the form of a cheque to the winner.

6 The winner will be the entrant who returns the reply card, or enters the prize promotion, and not necessarily the owner or purchaser of the Guide.

7 No purchase is necessary. To enter the prize promotion simply send a stamped self-addressed envelope to The Glove Box Guide Publishing Company at Barley House, Sopers Road, Cuffley EN6 4RY. All entries must be received by no later than 24th July 2005. A copy of the Guide will be allocated to the entrant and if this holds the winning number the entrant will receive the £500 prize and a bottle of champagne. Only one entry is allowed per person.

8 Your entry must be submitted with the correct postage to be eligible for entry.

9 The lucky number prize promotion is open to all UK residents over the age of 18, except for employees or associates of The Glove Box Guide Publishing Company and Sable Publishing or members of their immediate family.

10 The publishers reserve the right to feature the winner in all prize promotion-related publicity.

11 For the name of the winner, send a stamped, self-addressed envelope to The Glove Box Guide Publishing Company, Barley House, Sopers Road, Cuffley EN6 4RY by no later than 31st July 2005.

AFFIX
STAMP
HERE

The Glove Box Guide Publishing Company
Barley House
Sopers Road
Cuffley
Potters Bar
Hertfordshire
EN6 4RY

2004

Restaurant
& Pub
Guide

Your essential guide to over
a hundred of Hertfordshire's
most enjoyable places to eat

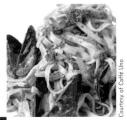

Courtesy of Caffé Uno

Courtesy of La Casetta

Recommendations you can trust

A
GLOVE
BOX
GUIDE

Publisher The Glove Box Guide Publishing Company
Barley House, Sopers Road, Cuffley
Potters Bar, Hertfordshire EN6 4RY
Telephone: 01707 876533
www.gloveboxguides.net
Email: info@gloveboxguides.net

Copyright HERTFORDSHIRE Restaurant & Pub Guide 2004
© The Glove Box Guide Publishing Company 2003

ISBN **0-9544816-0-7**

Design Baines Design, Potters Bar, Hertfordshire

Editorial Kevin Saunders

Print Unwin Brothers Ltd, Woking, Surrey

Distribution Sable Publishing, Potters Bar, Hertfordshire

Maps © Collins Bartholomew Ltd 2003
Reproduced by permission of Harper Collins Publishers
at www.bartholomewmaps.com

Contents

Courtesy of Loch Fyne Restaurant

Hertfordshire's towns

Welcome to the first edition of our essential guide to eating out in Hertfordshire.

With a vast array of restaurants and pubs across the county it's hard to know which ones to choose. Our GLOVE BOX GUIDE aims to help you make a good choice every time so keep it to hand in your glove box for easy reference.

Mystery diners have been eating out in Hertfordshire over the past year to ensure that you can eat out with confidence. Only those restaurants and pubs whose ambience, style, service and, of course, quality of cuisine met our high standards were invited to be featured.

The best however, isn't necessarily the most expensive. This Guide gives you detailed information about great places to eat that are perfect for every pocket and any occasion.

A unique feature of the Guide is the money-saving vouchers which offer concessions or discounts at the majority of the featured restaurants and pubs. These include, for example, a free bottle of wine or a discount on your bill.

It's not just the establishment that makes eating out enjoyable, it's the location too. And that's why each town has a preface with a brief introduction to its history and places of interest to visit.

Finally, stay up-to-date with news about eating out in Hertfordshire with our free four-monthly newsletter FOOD FOR THOUGHT.

Enjoy!

Courtesy of Nicholls Brasserie

Your experiences

We are always pleased to hear from our readers and to receive your comments about the restaurants and pubs featured in this Guide as well as others which you have visited in Hertfordshire.

If you have enjoyed a particularly good meal we would like to hear from you.

We expect the restaurants and pubs which are included in this Guide to maintain their high standards. If they fail to do so we would like to know.

To contact us, simply complete the comments form at the back of the Guide on page 167 or send an email to feedback@gloveboxguides.net

Thank you.

Courtesy of Hanbury Manor

FOOD FOR THOUGHT

FOOD FOR THOUGHT is our four-monthly newsletter.

It is a great way to keep up-to-date on the best places to eat out in Hertfordshire with essential news on new restaurants, new and changing menus, award winning restaurants and pubs together with news of local events and entertainment.

To ensure you receive your free copy of FOOD FOR THOUGHT complete and return the 'Lucky Number' form at the front of the Guide.

How to use the Guide

Average Price
The cost is based on an average three course evening meal excluding drinks. Please note that this is only a guide and we advise you to check the cost of your meal before you order.

Maps
Detailed maps are provided on pages 161-166 which show all the towns, villages and major roads in Hertfordshire.

Food style - not every restaurant falls neatly into a category so check the description for more detailed information.

(English/British) (Average Price: £17.50)

The Beehive
Epping Green (Map Ref: 165 F6)

Epping Green
Nr. Little Berkhamsted SG13 8NB
Tel: 01707 875959

A picturesque public house serving quality ales and excellent food – specialising in fish

Opening hours
M-F   11.30-2.30   5.30-11.00
Sat   11.30-3.00   6.00-11.00
Sun   12.00-5.00

Food served
M-F   12.00-2.00   7.00-9.00
Sat   12.00-2.30   7.00-9.00
Sun   12.00-4.00

Food style
English/British, specialising in fish

Index
Looking for something or somewhere in particular? Refer to the indexes on pages 144-160.

Features & facilities
Garden/Outside eating area
Non-smoking area
Real ales
Vegetarian dishes
Wheelchair access
Wines - good selection

Husband and wife Maurice and Marie offer a friendly welcome and over the past 5 years they have built a reputation for excellent food and very generous portions.

Specialising in fresh fish, the blackboard menu changes every day to offer the best from the market. Skate and crab are always popular choices. The menu also offers a varied selection of steaks, chicken and vegetarian dishes. If you're just after a quick bite, a full snack menu is available from the bar. The main eating area is now almost completely non-smoking.

The service is always friendly and efficient and the bar always offers a guest ale and a range of malt whiskies.

The woodburning stoves in the winter and the hanging baskets in the summer add to the ambience of this fine hostelry.

The pub is easy to find on the main road between Little Berkhamsted and Newgate Street and there is a large car park.

Concessionary vouchers
See information on the opposite page.

REDEMPTION
SIGNATURE

Free bottle of house wine
with a two course meal for table of 4, Mon-Thurs
See terms & conditions on page 7. Expiry date: 31 December 2004

6

Courtesy of The Waffle House

Terms and conditions of use for your vouchers

Courtesy of Hanbury Manor

Please do not remove the vouchers from the Guide.

- Your vouchers are only valid if you present the complete Guide to the restaurant before you order your meal.

- Each voucher can only be used on one occasion.

- A voucher is valid for up to four people when you order the minimum of a two course meal, unless otherwise stated or agreed.

- Each voucher clearly shows the concession or discount on offer, when it is valid and its expiry date.

Once a voucher has been used it will be initialled by the restaurant to confirm it has been redeemed.

Vouchers cannot be used in conjunction with any other offer or promotion and are invalid, unless otherwise agreed, on:
Bank Holidays, Valentine's Day, Mother's Day, Father's Day, Christmas Day, Boxing Day, New Year's Eve and New Year's Day.

Baldock

including the villages of Ashwell and Hinxworth

Founded in 1145 by the Knights Templar, the town's actual origins go back much further to a Roman settlement at the crossroads of the Roman roads of Icknield Way and Stane Street.

The smallest of the four towns in North Hertfordshire, Baldock is, nonetheless, a growing residential area. But it still retains much of the charm and interest you would expect from a market town that derived its prosperity from the coaching trade on the Great North Road. This is evident in its wide High Street and its wealth of ancient inns, such as the half-timbered 17th century Bull's Head Inn in Church Street. So it's no surprise, that Baldock is one of just five towns in Hertfordshire listed by the Council for British Archaeology as being of national importance.

One of Baldock's key architectural delights is the fine old Kayser Bonder stocking factory, which is now a local supermarket.

However, the 14th century church is undoubtedly the town's dominant feature with its embattled tower and 'spike', which ensures that it can be seen for many miles around. Among the church's many interesting features, one is particularly amusing and touching at the same time: the graveboard that says: 'How soon I was cut down, when innocent at play the wind it blew a scaffold down and took my Life away'.

The Great North Road in modern form is, of course, the A1(M) and, with direct rail connections to London King's Cross, Stevenage and Cambridge, Baldock is within easy reach of London and other key towns in Hertfordshire.

(Modern British)   (Average Price: £19.00)   Ashwell (Map Ref: 162 F2)

Mill Street
Ashwell, Nr Baldock SG7 5LY
Tel: 01462 742394

*Quality modern cuisine
in a stylish country pub
and restaurant*

Opening hours

M-F	11.30-3.00	6.00-11.00
Sat	11.30-3.00	6.00-11.00
Sun	12.00noon - 10.30pm	

Food served

M-F	12.00-2.30	6.30-9.30
Sat	12.00-2.30	6.30-9.30
Sun	12.00-4.00	7.00-9.30

Food style
Modern British and
European

Features & facilities
Child friendly
 - High chairs
 - Children's menu
Garden/Outside eating area
Non-smoking area
Real ales
Special diets catered for
Vegetarian dishes
Weddings/private functions
Wheelchair access
Wines - extensive selection

This delightful old English country inn boasts a welcoming and comfortable bar and a large stylish separate restaurant. Well positioned in the delightful village of Ashwell, it is very popular with walkers.

The building which now houses the stunning restaurant used to be a school hall in the 1930s and later a bowling alley. However, it is now very stylish, spacious and comfortable.

The menu is varied with inspiration taken from the best of British and European cuisines. All the produce is fresh, cooked to order and mostly sourced from local suppliers.

During the year a number of theme nights are held with menus focussing on, for example, Italian food, the 'Best of British Beef' and a seafood extravaganza.

The cosy bar area is always inviting with leather sofas you can just sink into. A selection of real ales including Adnams and Bombadier and often a choice of guest ales is available.

To the rear of the pub is a large garden with wooden benches and a large car park. The staff are always friendly, knowledgeable and efficient.

If you fancy a jaunt in the country, then this is a wonderful excuse.

Old White Horse

Baldock (Map Ref: **162** F2) (International) (Average Price: £20.00)

1 Station Road
Baldock SG7 5BS
Tel: 01462 893168
Fax: 01462 892980
www.oldwhitehorse.com

*Popular country inn
with an attractive,
contemporary feel*

Opening hours
M-Sa 11.00am - 11.00pm
Sun 11.00noon - 10.30pm

Food served
M-Sa 12.00-2.30 6.30-9.00
Sun June-August
12.00-3.00 BBQ from 3.00
September-May
12.00-3.00 6.00-8.30

Food style
International

Features & facilities
Child friendly
- High chairs
- Children's menu
Disabled facilities
Garden/Outside eating area
Non-smoking area
Private functions
Real ales
Special diets catered for
Vegetarian dishes
Wheelchair access
Wines - extensive selection

Situated on the main road which runs through the town, the Old White Horse is a traditional inn which was once a trading post with stabling at the rear.

Today this popular country pub is managed by licensee Margaret Patterson and her team of friendly, professional staff.

Refurbished two years ago, the pub has an attractive, contemporary feel, appealing to locals and visitors alike. Regular entertainment is provided with a folk night on Wednesdays, a live band on the first Friday of the month and special events such as Burns Night, St Georges Night and Beaujolais Nouveau celebrations.

The varied bar menu ensures no-one is disappointed with a special menu for OAPs and children. Alternatively, Rafters Restaurant provides a more cosmopolitan and comprehensive menu with daily specials to tempt the discerning diner.

The restaurant is open 7 days a week and provides the perfect venue for functions of up to 80 people.

REDEMPTION
SIGNATURE

**10% Discount
Monday-Friday**
See terms & conditions on page 7. Expiry date: 31 December 2004

Zeus Hotel & Restaurant

Greek | Average Price: £19.95

Baldock (Map Ref: 162 F2)

20 High Street
Baldock SG7 6AX
Tel: 01462 893620
Fax: 01462 892242
info@zeushotelandrestaurant.co.uk
www.zeushotelandrestaurant.co.uk

Excellent food, friendly staff, first class reputation

Opening hours

M-Th 7.00am - 11.00pm
Fri 8.00am - 1.00am
Sat 8.00am - 1.00am
Sun 8.00am - 3.30pm

Food served

M-F 7.00-2.00 5.30-10.30
Sat 8.00-2.00 7.00-10.00
Sun 12.00-3.00

Food style

Mainly Greek but with a range of English, British and Turkish as well seafood

Features & facilities

Garden/Outside eating area
Vegetarian dishes
Weddings/Private functions
Wines - extensive selection

This privately owned restaurant and hotel is set in the quaint market town of Baldock and has been run by the same owners for the last twenty years. The building is steeped in history. Built as a private house and maltings in the early 18th century its previous owners include the Ind family, founders of the Ind Coope brewery company.

The restaurant offers a wide selection of traditional Greek and English food prepared on the premises by one of their experienced chefs. The Chef's Meze is highly recommended – a selection of ten hot and cold dishes. To complement your meal select a wine from the varied and extensive list of Greek, Cypriot, French or new world wines.

Well established, the traditional Greek party nights on Fridays and Saturdays are always busy with upwards of 200 diners enjoying a traditional Greek meal with live music, belly dancers, impressionists and a disco.

REDEMPTION
SIGNATURE

10% discount (FOOD ONLY)
Monday - Thursday

See terms & conditions on page 7 Expiry date: 31 December 2004

The Three Horseshoes

Hinxworth (Map Ref: 162 F2)　　(English/British)　　(Average Price: £15.00)

High Street, Hinxworth
Baldock SG7 5HQ
Tel:　01462 742280
www.hinxworthpub.co.uk

Enjoy quality food and
drink in a warm and
comfortable atmosphere

Opening hours

M-F	11.30-3.00	6.00-11.00
Sat	11.30-3.00	6.00-11.00
Sun	12.00-3.00	7.00-10.30

Food served

M-F	12.00-2.00	7.00-9.00
Sat	12.00-2.00	7.00-9.00
Sun	12.00-2.00 only	

Food style
English/British

Features & facilities
Child friendly
 - High chairs
 - Children's menu
Garden/Outside eating area
Non-smoking area
Real ales
Special diets catered for
Vegetarian dishes
Wines - extensive selection

Geoff and Sharon Fiddler have run this popular pub for the past two years. However, the site itself has been a local watering hole since the 1700's.

The delightful thatched building is over 500 years old and is tucked away in the top most corner of the county. The thatched roof and exposed beams add to its ambience, as does the large woodburner, which is housed in a beautiful inglenook fireplace and is especially appealing on cold winter nights. The separate dining area overlooks the spacious garden and open countryside.

The extensive à la carte and bar menu are available for both lunch and dinner, every day except Sunday. The current choice includes a duo of poached and smoked salmon mousse to start, with perhaps slices of duck breast served in a rich port, cranberry and red onion sauce to follow and completed by a bramley apple and cinnamon pudding. There is always an excellent selection of fresh fish and a choice of vegetarian dishes available.

The tantalising range of wines, both new and old world, are available at very reasonable prices, or try one of the selection of real ales.

On summer nights, nothing is more appealing than sitting with friends in the idyllic garden.

THE THREE
HORSESHOES
PUBLIC HOUSE & RESTAURANT

Barnet

including Hadley Wood

Barnet Highlights

- The Royal Air Force Museum at Hendon

- The Church Farmhouse Museum at Hendon

- The London Museum of Jewish Life at The Sternberg Centre, Finchley

- Barnet Museum

- Coming soon for 2004 – the Artsdepot

On the southern borders of Hertfordshire, Barnet is one of the London boroughs where the home counties meets London. Barnet was built alongside Watling Street, the Romans' major route from London to the north.

Hadley Green, in the north of the Borough, was the centre of the bloody Battle of Barnet in 1471 when the Yorkists defeated the Lancastrians during the War of the Roses. More recently, Hendon, in the south of the borough, played host to the pioneers of aviation when Claude Grahame-White founded his airport and staged daring public displays until the airfield was eventually requisitioned in the war and sold to the Royal Air Force.

That airborne heritage is still in evidence today at Hendon's famous Royal Air Force Museum, while Barnet Museum offers bloodcurdling mementoes of the Battle of Barnet. The London Museum of Jewish life in Finchley opens a window on another vital part of the area's history – the religious and working lives of the Jewish community.

Barnet is packed with activity, from the excellent sports amenities at the Copthall Sports Centre in Mill Hill, the three public golf courses and the Welsh Harp sailing lake to the exciting programme of arts at the Bull Theatre, art gallery and studio in High Barnet.

And the stage is set for the opening in 2004 of Artsdepot – a world-class cultural and entertainments centre at Tally Ho corner in Finchley with plans for shops and a health and leisure centre as well as a wide range of entertainments.

Information kindly provided by the London Borough of Barnet

Grittz

Barnet (Map Ref: **165** F7)

(Italian) (Average Price: £14.00)

135 High Street
Barnet
Tel: 020 8275 9985

Grittz boasts the only wood burning stove in the area

Opening hours
M-F 12.00 noon - 11.00pm
Sat 12.00 noon - 11.00pm
Sun 12.00 noon - 11.00pm

Food served
M-F 12.00 noon - 10.45pm
Sat 12.00 noon - 10.45pm
Sun 12.00 noon - 10.45pm

Food style
Italian

Features & facilities
Child friendly
- High chairs
- Children's menu
Disabled facilities
Non-smoking area
Private functions
Vegetarian dishes
Wheelchair access

Grittz is run like a family business and the whole family is very welcome. The atmosphere is always friendly and relaxed, children are welcome and high chairs are always available.

The interior is bright and stylish and great for a quick lunch or leisurely dinner. Grittz boasts the only wood burning oven in the area and serves superb pizzas complemented by a full range of Mediterranean style dishes. There is also a full range of grilled meat, chicken, fish dishes and daily specials on offer.

The lunchtime deal of any pizza and an ice cream for £5 is excellent value and the prompt service is a real bonus if your time is limited.

The restaurant is fully licenced and bookings are recommended, though not essential, at weekends. Open for two years, this restaurant deserves its local reputation for quality and value - and great pizzas.

REDEMPTION
SIGNATURE

Free bottle of house wine
per table of 4, Mon to Thurs evenings

See terms & conditions on page 7 Expiry date: 31 December 2004

14

Cedar Restaurant, West Lodge Park Hotel

(Modern English) (Average Price: £24.95)   Hadley Wood (Map Ref: 165 F7)

Cockfosters Road
Hadley Wood, Nr Barnet EN4 0PY
Tel: 020 8216 3900
Fax: 020 8216 3937
westlodgepark@bealeshotels.co.uk
www.bealeshotels.co.uk

*A perfect place for that
special occasion*

Opening hours

M-F	12.30-2.00	7.00-9.30
Sat	Closed lunchtime	
	7.00-10.00	
Sun	12.15-2.30	7.00-9.00

Food style
Modern British

Features & facilities
Child friendly
- High chairs
Garden/Outside eating area
Non-smoking area
Weddings/private functions
Wheelchair access
Wines - extensive selection

Other hotel facilities:
59 bedrooms (inc four poster)
8 conference rooms
Putting green, croquet lawn
Helipad
Golf practice net
Beauty rooms
Hot tub & sauna

The Beale family has owned West Lodge Park Hotel since 1945. The Hotel is set in 35 acres of parkland and includes the Beale Arboretum which contains over 600 different species of shrubs and trees.

The Cedar Restaurant overlooks these beautiful grounds and it is hard to believe that central London is just 20 minutes' away. A perfect place for that special occasion, the cuisine is 'modern British', stylishly presented and complemented by an extensive wine list from around the world.

There is a regular programme of special events including concerts and gourmet dinners. Party nights are held during December. Morning coffee, light refreshments and afternoon teas are also popular and are served in the bar and lounge.

All the bedrooms have garden or country views and the hotel contains family portraits, open fires and antique furniture. The bar is open to non-residents and the terrace provides a relaxing place to enjoy a chilled glass of wine or Pimms.

REDEMPTION
SIGNATURE

10% Discount
Mon-Fri lunch & dinner or Sunday dinner

See terms & conditions on page 7. Expiry date: 31 December 2004

Spizzico

Barnet (Map Ref: **165** F7)

(Italian) (Average Price: £18.00)

196 High Street
Barnet EN5 5SZ
Tel: 020 8440 2255
www.spizzicorestaurant.co.uk

*Predominantly Italian
but with a unique mix
of American dishes*

Opening hours
M-F 12.00 noon-12.00midnight
Sat 12.00 noon-12.00midnight
Sun 12.00 noon-12.00midnight

Food style
A mix of Italian, American
and Mexican

Features & facilities
Child friendly
- High chairs
- Children's menu
Disabled facilities
Non-smoking area
Private functions
Special diets catered for
Vegetarian dishes
Wheelchair access
Wines - extensive selection

This contemporary restaurant, set in the heart of
Barnet, opened nearly four years ago.

Open from noon to midnight every day,
Spizzico is a great choice whether you simply
want a coffee, a light snack or a meal.

The cuisine is predominantly Italian but with a
unique mix of American and Mexican dishes
such as the sizzling fajitas made with a choice
of chicken, beef, jumbo prawn or a vegetarian
option. Everything is freshly cooked using only
the finest ingredients and the range of pizzas
and pastas are also popular choices. The menu
is complemented by a good wine list.

Spizzico has tiled floors, solid wood tables,
subtle lighting and modern art and there is
always a modern display of fresh flowers on the
bar to complete the stylish effect. Weather
permitting, the French doors are kept open
which gives a continental feel to the restaurant.

Spizzico also has a bar licence so you are
welcome just to pop in just for a drink. The
staff are always friendly and welcoming.

Loch Fyne Restaurant

12 Hadley Highstone
Barnet EN5 4PU
Tel: 020 8449 3674
Fax: 020 8441 6342

*Great seafood in
relaxed and friendly
surroundings*

Opening hours

M-F 9.00am - 10.00pm
Sat 10.00am - 10.30pm
Sun 10.00am - 9.30pm

Food style

Fish/Seafood

Features & facilities

Child friendly
 - High chairs
Garden/Outside eating area
Non-smoking area
Private functions
Vegetarian dishes
Wines - extensive selection

Loch Fyne Restaurant brings Scotland's finest seafood to Hadley Highstone, Barnet.

The interior of the restaurant is warm and inviting with wooden furniture and flooring and an eclectic selection of art and artifacts that reflect the heritage of the company. A focal point is the large marble seafood counter displaying the fresh lobsters, oysters, mussels and white fish that form part of the extensive menu. This produce is also available for sale to non-diners who are looking for delicious, fresh seafood to prepare at home.

The menu is based on a selection of hot and cold dishes including classics such as mussels marinieres, lobster platter and a variety of white fish and special dishes created on the day. Much of the produce comes direct from Loch Fyne in Scotland where 'home grown' mussels and oysters are collected daily and delivered fresh to the restaurant along with smoked salmon products from the famous Loch Fyne Smokehouse.

Try the new grill menu which includes delicious meat dishes such as Glen Fyne beef sourced from local Scottish suppliers.

LOCH FYNE
RESTAURANTS LTD

REDEMPTION
SIGNATURE

Free glass of wine
with every main course

See terms & conditions on page 7. Expiry date: 31 December 2004

Publishers note: the photos depicted were not taken at the Barnet restaurant

Emchai

Barnet (Map Ref: 165 F7) (Oriental) (Average Price: £14.00)

78 High Street
Barnet EN5 5SN
Tel: 020 8364 9993
Fax: 020 8364 8333
www.emchai.co.uk

*If you enjoy oriental
cuisine then this is
certainly a place to try*

Opening hours

M-Th 12.00-2.30 6.00-11.00
Fri   12.00-2.30 6.00-12.00
Sat   12.00-3.00 6.00-12.00
Sun   12.00-3.00 5.00-10.00

Food style
Oriental, specialising in
Malaysian

Features & facilities
Child friendly
 - High chairs
Disabled facilities
Non-smoking area
Special diets catered for
Vegetarian dishes
Wheelchair access
Wines - extensive selection

One of the best oriental restaurants outside
central London, the predominately Malaysian
cuisine at Emchai is beautifully prepared and
presented.

The minimalist style, contemporary furniture
and crisp lighting all serve to enhance the
relaxed and informal atmosphere. Even the
chopsticks are stylish, carved from a single
piece of wood which you break in two.

All the food is freshly cooked and prepared on
the premises – you can watch the chefs at
work in the open plan kitchen.

Just to tempt you, try gado gado - a popular
Indonesian salad topped with peanut sauce, or
beef rendang - a Malaysian style dish cooked
in spicy coconut gravy.

The service is friendly and efficient without
being rushed.

The restaurant has been established for four
years and over that time has built up a well
deserved reputation for quality and service and
a loyal local following.

If you enjoy oriental cuisine then this is
certainly a place to try.

Caffè Uno

(Italian)   (Average Price: £15.00)

Barnet (Map Ref: 165 F7)

238-240 High Street
Barnet EN5 5DT
Tel: 020 8441 6112
Fax: 020 84407114
www.caffeuno.co.uk

*Warm and welcoming at
any time of the day – all
the food at Caffè Uno is
cooked to order*

Opening hours

M-Th 10.00-11.00 **Fri** to 11.30
Sat   10.00-11.30
Sun   11.00-10.30

Food served

M-F   10.00-11.00
Sat   10.00-11.30
Sun   11.00-10.00

Food style

Italian

Features & facilities

Child friendly
- High chairs
- Children's menu
Disabled facilities
Garden/Outside eating area
Non-smoking area
Private functions
Special diets catered for
Vegetarian dishes
Wheelchair access
Wines - extensive selection

Situated at the far end of the High Street in an
intimate location with a superb outside patio
area, Caffè Uno in Barnet is a warm and
friendly Italian restaurant.

All the food is cooked to order, from
mouthwatering grilled meat and fish dishes, to
a great selection of tasty pasta and delicious
thin crust pizzas. The chef also creates weekly
blackboard specials offering even more choice
and variety for the loyal Caffè Uno regular.

Quality is a passion at Caffè Uno and you'll
find that passion every day. It is open from
breakfast 'til late seven days a week. Perfect
for that morning cup of latte, ideal for lunch
and great for dinner, it's the perfect place to
go at any time.

A warm welcome is guaranteed.

CAFFÈ UNO

REDEMPTION
SIGNATURE

2 Free bottles of wine
for tables of 6 or more

See terms & conditions on page 7. Expiry date: 31 December 2004

Publishers note: the photos depicted were not taken at the Barnet restaurant

The Palace

Barnet (Map Ref: **165** F7)

(**Greek**) (**Average Price: £16.00**)

32 Station Road
New Barnet EN5 1QW
Tel: 020 8441 7192
Fax: 020 8441 7193

*A family run Greek
restaurant - a stylish,
friendly and relaxed
dining experience*

Opening hours

M-Th 12.00-3.00   6.00-12.00
Fr-Sat 12.00-3.00   6.00-1.00am
Sun 1.00pm - 12midnight

Food orders

M-Th 12.00-2.30   6.00-10.30
Fr-Sat 12.00-2.30   6.00-11.00
Sun 1.00pm - 10.00pm

Food style

Greek with a range of other
dishes from home and
abroad.

Features & facilities

Child friendly
 - High chairs
 - Children's menu
Disabled facilities
Garden/Outside eating area
Non-smoking area
Private functions
Vegetarian dishes
Wheelchair access
Wines - extensive selection

This restaurant is fairly new to Barnet but Mario,
Demi and their team have already established a
strong local following.

Set in the former Town Hall, the restaurant is
stylish with a mosaic tiled entrance, stripped
wooden floors, plain walls and a prominent
feature staircase. Outside are table and chairs
where you can eat or enjoy a pre-dinner drink
continental style!

All the staff are very friendly and help to create
the relaxed atmosphere in this busy restaurant.

The food is wonderful, all freshly cooked with a
wide variety of traditional Greek and
Mediterranean dishes. To sample a selection, try
the Meze, a feast of starters, meat and fish dishes
completed with a platter of fresh fruit. The
portions are very generous and at £16.00 per
head it's excellent value.

On offer is an extensive and reasonably priced
wine list, including a selection of Greek and
Cypriot wines.

There's something here for everyone and it
deserves to be popular.

REDEMPTION
SIGNATURE

**Free bottle of wine up to £15.00
for tables of 4, Sun-Thurs**

See terms & conditions on page 7. Expiry date: 31 December 2004

20

Berkhamsted

Dating back to medieval times, historic Berkhamsted nestles at the foot of the Chiltern Hills, drawing its life and vitality from the convergence of the Grand Union Canal, turnpike and railway. The town's origins are still evident in the ruins of Berkhamsted castle, complete with moat and grounds. In the nearby town centre, the early 13th century parish church and 15th century courthouse stamp their authority on the High Street.

The town also has illustrious literary connections and former residents include JM Barrie, author of Peter Pan, William Cowper, who coined the phrase 'God moves in a mysterious way' and Graham Greene, who is commemorated by the Graham Greene Birthplace Trust, which hosts an exciting international festival in his honour every autumn.

There are plenty of places to eat and relax in the town to suit every taste whilst you enjoy the local scenery. An after lunch stroll is rewarded by an excellent selection of antique shops, fashion boutiques and the bustling outdoor market.

The delights of the Grand Union canal towpath and the astounding views from the top of the monument to the Earl of Bridgewater (the 'Canal Duke') at nearby Ashridge, land owned by the National Trust with its burgeoning herds of deer are also on your doorstep.

Information kindly provided by the Dacorum Information Centre

Caffé Uno

Berkhamsted (Map Ref: 164 C6) 〔 Italian 〕 〔 Average Price: £15.00 〕

196 High Street
Berkhamsted HP4 3BA
Tel: 01442 874856
Fax: 01442 874947
www.caffeuno.co.uk

*Warm and welcoming at
any time of the day – all
the food at Caffé Uno is
cooked to order*

Opening hours
M-Th 10.00-11.00 **Fri** to 11.30
Sat   10.00-11.30
Sun   11.00-10.00

Food served
M-Th 12.00-10.45 **Fri** to 11.30
Sat   12.00-11.15
Sun   12.00-9.45

Food style
Italian

Features & facilities
Child friendly
 - High chairs
 - Children's menu
Disabled facilities
Garden/Outside eating area
Non-smoking area
Private functions
Special diets catered for
Vegetarian dishes
Wheelchair access
Wines - extensive selection

With a fantastic central location in the old Town Hall building, Caffé Uno in Berkhamsted is a delightful, warm and welcoming Italian restaurant with a real Tuscan kitchen atmosphere. Warm red brick and soft yellow walls with chunky wooden furniture and with fresh vegetables and flavoured oils on display combine to create a charming, relaxing environment at all times of the day.

All the food at Caffé Uno is cooked to order, from mouthwatering grilled meat and fish dishes, to a great selection of tasty pasta and delicious thin crust pizzas. The head chef also creates weekly blackboard specials offering seasonal dishes and even more choice.

Quality is a passion at Caffé Uno and you'll find that passion every day. It is open from breakfast 'til late seven days a week. Perfect for that morning cup of latte, ideal for lunch and great for dinner, it's the perfect place to go at any time. A warm welcome is always guaranteed.

CAFFÉ UNO

22

Publishers note: the photos depicted were not taken at the Berkhamsted restaurant

Nicholls Brasserie

(Modern European)   (Average Price: £21.50)   **Berkhamsted** (Map Ref: **164** C6)

163-165 High Street
Berkhamsted HP4 3HB
Tel: 01442 879988
Fax: 01442 879977
www.nichollsonline.com

*The Nicholl's team are
proud of their food
quality and excellent
customer service*

Opening hours

M-F	10.00-2.30 (last orders)
	6.30-10.00 (last orders)
Sat	10.00-10.00 (last orders)
Sun	10.30-8.30 (last orders)

Food style
Modern European

Features & facilities
Air conditioned
Child friendly
- Baby changing facilities
- High chairs
Conservatory
Live jazz on Sundays
Non-smoking area
Outside eating area
Vegetarian dishes
Wines - extensive selection

Since opening its doors in Berkhamsted in 1997, Nicholls Brasserie has maintained its popularity with satisfied local customers returning for great food and wine.

Situated in a charismatic Grade II listed building on the bustling High Street, this charming restaurant is warm and welcoming with low beams and quaint corners offering a degree of intimacy.

From 10.30am, delicious breakfast options are available. The main menu has a varied choice of freshly prepared dishes in a modern, contemporary style. There is also a daily choice of imaginative 'chef's specials' such as rosemary crust brie with beetroot, thai fish brochettes and lamb gigot marinated in honey and mint.

Nicholls Brasseries are renowned for their Sea Blackboards offering whole or fillets of fresh fish cooked lightly on the griddle with the chef's butter of the day. Shellfish is always available with dishes such as king prawns, mussels in white wine, garlic and chilli or fresh dressed crab.

With all day opening at the weekends, families and friends are welcomed to relax and enjoy the comfortable surroundings. Sundays are great with all day brunch and the in-house jazz band playing in the evening. Booking is advisable at the weekend.

Bishop's Stortford

including the village of Spellbrook

Bishop's Stortford Highlights

- The Rhodes Arts Complex

- The Bishop's Stortford Museum

- The Corn Exchange

For more information on the town and surrounding villages contact:

Bishop's Stortford TIC
The Old Monastery, Windhill,
Bishop's Stortford CM23 2ND
Tel: 01279 655831
Fax: 01279 653136
Email: tic@bishopsstortford.org

Opening hours:
Mon–Fri 9.00am - 5.00pm
Sat   9.00am - 1.00pm
Closed Sundays and Bank Holidays

Information kindly provided by
Bishop's Stortford Tourist
Information Centre

Straddling the River Stort near the border between the counties of Hertfordshire and Essex, Bishop's Stortford is often assumed to take its name after its ancient river crossing. But, in fact, the name 'Stort' only came into use in the late 16th century.

The town grew up at the ford where the Roman road from St Albans to Colchester crossed the river known as Esterteferde and this was probably named after a small clan who controlled the crossing.

Much later, around 1060, the town of Esterteferde, complete with its castle, was sold to the Bishops of London – hence the name Bishop's Esterteferd.

Its connection with London, not to mention Cambridge, Colchester and Newmarket, was reinforced by the arrival of the first mail coaches and then the railway.

To this day Bishop's Stortford attracts shoppers from miles around. As well as an intriguing range of specialist shops and the famous high street names, the town has a thriving market on Thursdays and Saturdays – just as it has for several centuries.

Stansted Airport is only seven miles away and with direct rail services to Liverpool Street station in London, and good local road connections to the A10 and M11, the town is easily accessible from almost anywhere.

Host

4 The Corn Exchange
Market Square
Bishop's Stortford CM23 3UU
Tel: 01279 657000
Fax: 01279 655566
www.hostrestaurant.co.uk

*A chic restaurant serving
a fusion of cusines from
around the world*

Opening hours

M-F	12.00noon - 11.00pm
Sat	12.00noon - 11.00pm
Sun	12.00noon - 11.00pm

Food served

M-F	12.00-3.00 6.00-10.00
Sat	12.00-3.00 6.00-10.00
Sun	1.00pm - 9.00pm

Food style
International

Features & facilities
Child friendly
Disabled facilities
Garden/Outside eating area
Non-smoking area
Private functions
Special diets catered for
Vegetarian dishes
Wines - extensive selection

This stunning restaurant has been open for three years. Set in the old corn exchange the historic façade contrasts with the modern chic interior, which has a surprisingly nautical feel.

The kitchen is open plan so you can watch the chefs at work whilst you enjoy your meal.

The food is described as 'modern British with world fusion'. Classic French sits comfortably alongside a modern twist on Vietnamese, Thai and Indian dishes. It's reasonably priced and the al fresco menu served on the terrace is just £12.50 for two courses.

The high ceilings in the restaurant give a wonderful feeling of space but not as much as the roof terrace which can seat 150 people and has superb views over the surrounding streets and across town. The area is covered and patio heaters keep away the early evening chill.

Smoking is permitted in the bar area but not in the restaurant.

The selection of wines is generous, with up to 15 wines offered by the glass. There is also a choice of cocktails and an unusually exotic selection of beers and ales.

Entertainment is provided on Tuesday nights with live acoustic sets.

The Three Horseshoes

Spellbrook (Map Ref: 163 I4)   (English/British)   (Average Price: £15.00)

Spellbrook Lane East
Spellbrook, Bishop's Stortford
CM22 7SE
Tel: 01279 722849
Fax: 01279 600149

The chalkboards offer an amazing array of freshly cooked food

Opening hours

M-F   11.00am - 11.00pm
Sat   11.00am - 11.00pm
Sun   12.00noon - 10.30pm

Food served

M-F   12.00noon - 10.00pm
Sat   12.00noon - 10.00pm
Sun   12.00noon - 9.00pm

Food style

English/British

Features & facilities

Child friendly
 - High chairs
Disabled facilities
Garden/Outside eating area
Non-smoking area
Private functions
Real ales
Vegetarian dishes
Wheelchair access
Wines - extensive selection

Tucked away off the main road between Bishop's Stortford and Sawbridgeworth this deceptively large pub is open all day, every day.

The Three Horseshoes exudes the character and charm of a traditional British pub with a quaint exterior, part barn-style and part thatched and an inviting interior.

Situated on the bank of the Spellbrook stream, the building dates back to medieval times when it was probably a farm dwelling. The pub was first listed in 1899 as a beerhouse and has been a popular watering hole ever since.

The chalkboards offer an amazing choice of freshly cooked food, created and prepared by a skilled team of chefs using the finest ingredients. Fresh fish is a house speciality but whatever you choose it's prepared with the same commitment and enthusiasm so you're unlikely to be disappointed.

The choice of hand-pulled fine ales and wines from around the world is excellent and good value for money.

Part of the Chef and Brewer chain of pubs it really has a welcoming, relaxed and homely feel. Whether you're looking for a quiet meal in a cosy corner or a big Sunday lunch with all the family this is definitely a place to try.

Caffé Uno

Bishop's Stortford (Map Ref: 163 I4)

2/4 North Street
Bishop's Stortford CM23 2LQ
Tel: 01279 755725
Fax: 01279 757335
www.caffeuno.co.uk

*Warm and welcoming at
any time of the day – all
the food at Caffé Uno is
cooked to order*

Opening hours
M-F 10.00-11.00
Sat 10.00-11.30
Sun 11.00-10.30

Food served
M-F 12.00-11.00
Sat 10.00-11.30
Sun 11.00-10.30

Food style
Italian

Features & facilities
Child friendly
 - High chairs
 - Children's menu
Disabled facilities
Non-smoking area
Private functions
Special diets catered for
Vegetarian dishes
Wheelchair access

This is a warm and friendly Italian restaurant with a vibrant atmosphere centrally located in the town. Recently refurbished, the restaurant has a real Tuscan kitchen feel. Warm red brick and soft yellow walls with chunky wooden furniture and with fresh vegetables and flavoured oils on display combine to create a charming, relaxing environment at all times of the day.

All the food at Caffé Uno is cooked to order, from a great selection of grilled meat and fish dishes to tasty pasta dishes and delicious thin crust pizzas. The chef also creates weekly blackboard specials offering even more choice and variety for the loyal Caffé Uno regular.

Quality is a passion at Caffé Uno and you'll find that passion every day. It is open from breakfast 'til late seven days a week. Perfect for that morning cup of latte, ideal for lunch and great for dinner, it's the perfect place to go at any time. A warm welcome is guaranteed.

CAFFÉ UNO

27

The Lemon Tree

Bishop's Stortford (Map Ref: **163** I4)   (Modern European)   (Average Price: £25.00)

14-16 Water Lane
Bishop's Stortford CM23 4RL
Tel: 01279 757788
Fax: 01279 757766
mail@lemontree.co.uk
www.lemontree.co.uk

*A deserved reputation for
extremely high standards
in food and service*

Opening hours

Tu-F 12.00-2.30 (last orders)
7.00-9.30 (last orders)
Sat 12.30-2.30 (last orders)
7.00-9.30 (last orders)
Sun 1.00-4.00 (last orders)

Food style
Modern European

Features & facilities
Child friendly
- High chairs
Disabled facilities
Non-smoking area
Special diets catered for
Vegetarian dishes
Weddings/Private functions
Wheelchair access
Wines - extensive selection

The Lemon Tree is the concept of head chef Luke Fishpool, with support from his wife and co-proprietor Sue, who takes care of front-of-house. Since opening in 1996 the restaurant has established a reputation for extremely high standards in food and service.

Situated in an attractive Georgian terrace a few steps away from the main town centre, the restaurant occupies a listed building with exposed beams and fireplaces. A new bar/lounge has a modern informal appearance for guests to meet in a pleasant and comfortable environment.

The menu provides a variety of six or seven starters and main courses in a modern European style, from seared wild sea bass, cherry tomato and borlotti bean vierge to grilled calf's liver, bacon mash and onion gravy. A full à la carte menu is available in the evenings with a mid-week set menu offering exceptional value. The lunch programme's '7lt' is a one course meal from a selection of seven dishes with a glass of wine and filter coffee for £7.00. This option runs alongside the 2 or 3 course lunch menu.

There is an extensive wine list. Recently the choice of wines by the glass has increased and a range of cognacs and malt whiskies has been introduced. Seasonal wines are promoted throughout the year.

Borehamwood and Elstree

Borehamwood is a lively, modern town within easy reach of London to the south, yet surrounded by attractive Green Belt countryside. Until the middle of the 19th century it was a small rural hamlet but the construction of the Midland Railway in 1868 and the subsequent opening of Elstree Station changed the area forever. Borehamwood began to boom, boosted by an influx of manufacturing industry triggered by the outbreak of the First World War and later by the opening of the Barnet bypass in 1927.

But Borehamwood is best known for its starring role in the international film industry as the 'British Hollywood'. The movie industry has brought employment and economic growth to the area – not to mention a touch of glamour.

The town may not quite have the kudos of tinseltown but nevertheless the roll call of stars who have graced the Elstree Studios is impressive! The Hollywood imports include Grace Kelly, Errol Flynn, Sophia Loren and Cary Grant. The British names are no less notable and include Elizabeth Taylor, Laurence Olivier, John Mills, Alec Guinness and Ralph Richardson, to name but a few.

More recently, the Star Wars trilogy was filmed in the Studios, as were Spielberg's Indiana Jones adventures starring Harrison Ford. Perhaps the most familiar of all the faces though who are regularly spotted in Borehamwood, are those of the Eastenders cast whose 'Albert Square' is part of the BBC studios set within Elstree, and which is open for public tours.

Signor Baffi

Borehamwood (Map Ref: **165** E7)　　　(Italian)　(Average Price: £20.00)

195 Shenley Road
Borehamwood
Tel: 020 8953 8404
www.signorbaffi.co.uk

*An unforgettable
experience you will want
to enjoy again and again*

Opening hours

M-F　12.00-3.00　7.00-11.00
Sat　12.00-3.00　7.00-11.00
Sun　Closed

Food served

M-F　12.00-2.30　7.00-10.30
Sat　12.00-2.30　7.00-10.30
Sun　Closed

Food style
Italian

Features & facilities
Child friendly
 - High chairs
Disabled facilities
Non-smoking area
Private functions
Vegetarian dishes
Wheelchair access
Wines - extensive selection

Signor Baffi's in Borehamwood is close to the famous Elstree Film Studios and BBC TV Studios and is a favourite venue for star spotting.

Established some thirty years ago it is now owned by David Da Costa and its popularity is at its height. It has been extensively refurbished and and has a very friendly and comfortable atmosphere, which is enhanced by the good humour of the staff.

Manager for the last 13 years, Silvano Gaibani is the ever charming, welcoming face of the restaurant who will ensure your dining experience is as relaxing and enjoyable as possible.

The extensive menu is regularly revised and includes the finest Italian and continental cuisine, including fish and vegetarian dishes, together with daily specials. It is complemented by a well-stocked wine cellar, consisting of fine and affordable Italian wines.

The restaurant is available for private functions and it is happy to cater for all needs. Sundays are reserved for private functions.

Cavendish Restaurant, Edgwarebury Hotel

(English/British)   (Average Price: £25.00)   **Elstree** (Map Ref: **165** E7)

Barnet Lane
Elstree WD6 3RE
Tel: 0870 609 6151
Fax: 020 8207 3668
edgwarebury@corushotels.com
www.corushotels.com/edgwarebury

Excellent cuisine
complimented by a wide
ranging wine list

Opening hours

M-F   11.00am - 11.00pm
Sat   Closed
Sun   12.00noon - 10.30pm

Food served

M-F   12.30-2.15   7.00-9.30
Sat   7.00-9.30
Sun   12.30-2.30   7.00-9.15

Food style
British with continental
influence

Features & facilities
Child friendly
 - High chairs
Garden/Outside eating area
Vegetarian dishes
Wines - extensive selection

The Edgwarebury Hotel and rosette rated Cavendish Restaurant offer a homely country house atmosphere. Steeped in character with its charming Tudor style exterior, the hotel stands on the site of an old house dating back to 1540, set in beautiful landscaped gardens surrounded by 10 acres of natural woodland.

Relax with your favourite drink and enjoy the informal atmosphere of the Terrace bar. Feast your eyes on the beautiful antiquities throughout and enjoy the stunning views over central London from the outer Terrace.

Savour the excellent cuisine complimented by a wide ranging wine list in the intimate and characterful Cavendish Restaurant. Alternatively, you can dine on the terrace during the summer months or enjoy your own special function in the unique ambience of the private dining rooms. The range of menus throughout the day starts with breakfast and progresses to the lounge menu, the business lunch menu and an extensive dinner menu. Advance reservations are essential.

And, as a long standing favourite of Elstree Film Studios and the BBC, who knows which celebrity you might bump into when you dine here!

REDEMPTION
SIGNATURE

One free bottle of house wine
for tables of 4 or more, Sunday to Friday evenings and Sunday lunch

See terms & conditions on page 7. Expiry date: 31 December 2004

31

Broxbourne

Broxbourne Highlights

- Paradise Wildlife Park

- Broxbourne Woods

- St Augustine's Church

- The Old Manor House, Baas Hill

As its coat of arms suggests, Broxbourne is a town with an enduring affection for badgers – its name is derived from the Saxon Broc (badger) and combined with Bourne (stream).

The town has come a long way since its mention in the Domesday Book as Brochesborne and it has grown considerably. Nevertheless, the badgers so close to its heart are still very much in evidence, partly because the beautiful Broxbourne Woods to the north are still so well-preserved and a joy to take a stroll in. And if any further proof was needed that the town's affinity for badgers is alive and kicking, you need look no further than the purpose-built badger tunnel under the busy A10, designed to reduce badger road deaths!

Many of Broxbourne's older buildings have been lost to recent development but a few notable examples remain, such as the 1728 Monson Almshouses built by the Monsons of Broxbournebury, which is now a special school. Among numerous notables of the town are the elder brother of Christian Fletcher of 'Mutiny on the Bounty' fame and John McAdam, the tarmac pioneer, who is commemorated in the St Augustine's church as 'the great improver of British roads'.

Once a mere adjunct to the Hoddesdon parish, Broxbourne now rivals its neighbour for entertainment, leisure and sports facilities with the ever-popular Broxbourne Lido, the vast Lea Valley Park, Paradise Wildlife Park in Broxbourne Woods and a packed entertainment agenda at Broxbourne Civic Hall.

Washington Restaurant, Cheshunt Marriott Hotel

(International) (Average Price: £18.00)   Turnford (Map Ref: **166** G6)

Halfhide Lane
Turnford EN10 6NG
Tel: 01992 451245
Fax: 01992 461611
www.marriott.co.uk/stnch

A 'home from home'
setting - a popular venue
for breakfast, lunch or
dinner'

Opening hours

M-F Breakfast 6.30-11.00
Lunch 12.00-2.30
Dinner 5.00-10.00

Sa/Su Breakfast 7.00-11.00
Lunch 12.00-2.30
Dinner 5.00-10.00

Food style
International

Features & facilities
Child friendly
- High chairs
- Children's menu
Disabled facilities
Non-smoking area
Special diets catered for
Vegetarian dishes
Weddings/Private functions
Wheelchair access
Wines - extensive selection

The 'home from home' setting of the Washington Restaurant offers breakfast, lunch and dinner to residents and non-residents. The breakfast buffet offers a wide selection of English and Continental buffet items. Lunch is a fixed price menu and the à la carte dinner menu offers items from succulent prime steaks to the very popular Marriott Burger!

At the weekend, experience a traditional Sunday lunch, with either a two or three course carvery. Book early to avoid disappointment.

The Washington's lounge is a popular venue for snacks and light bites making it the perfect setting for a speedy lunch. The relaxed atmosphere of their fireplace area is the ideal location for small weddings and family celebrations.

The Cheshunt Marriott Hotel also offers four star accommodation and conference facilities.

REDEMPTION
SIGNATURE

Complimentary bottle of wine
for table of 4 adults - any day, lunch or dinner

See terms & conditions on page 7. Expiry date: 31 December 2004

33

The Highland Restaurant

Broxbourne (Map Ref: **166** G6) (Greek) (Average Price: £20.00)

9-11 The Precinct
High Road
Broxbourne
Tel: 01992 466933

The food is predominantly Greek but a full range of steaks and other dishes are also on offer

Opening hours

M-F	12.00-2.30	6.00-late
Sat	Closed	6.00-late
Sun	12.00-4.30	Closed

Food served

M-F	12.00-2.00	6.00-11.00
Sat	Closed	6.00-11.00
Sun	12.00-2.30	Closed

Food style
Greek

Features & facilities
Child friendly
Disabled facilities
Special diets catered for
Weddings/private functions
Wheelchair access
Wines - extensive selection

The Highland Restaurant is a modern Greek restaurant and steak house in the heart of Broxbourne.

It has been run by the same family for the last 14 years and has built up a good reputation for serving quality food with friendly service and a great atmosphere.

Inside, the restaurant is stylish with wood panelled walls, modern pictures and mirrors, crisp linen table cloths and smart linen napkins. The large open plan eating area is great for groups or small parties and there is also a small bar area where you can enjoy a drink before your meal.

The food is predominantly Greek but a full range of steaks and other dishes are also on offer so there is something for everyone. The friendly staff are always willing to offer advice on the Greek and Cypriot menu. One of the most popular dishes is 'yiacoumi', which is a traditional Cypriot dish of slow cooked lamb.

The wine list includes a number of popular Greek and Cypriot wines and is reasonably priced.

Every six weeks there is a Greek party night with traditional table dancing, belly dancers and plate smashing which are always lively events enjoyed by all.

Buntingford

including the villages of Brent Pelham, Cottered and Westmill

Buntingford Highlights

- Jubilee Pump

- Town Clock

- Ward's Hospital

- St Peter's Church

Rural but far from remote, Buntingford's historical heart is agricultural but, still to this day, the town's lifeblood is the busy A10 - the Roman Ermine Street. In fact, the settlement itself was called 'Ermine Street' as late as the 17th century. Today, however, the easy road connections to Cambridge and London make the town's outlying industrial parks as vital to its life as the farms.

Although the town's sign features a bunting, it's not named after this pretty indigenous bird. In fact, the town's name is more likely to have come from an ancient local tribe: the Bunta.

As a market town Buntingford has always been something of a local hub. But it was the rise of coach travel in Elizabethan times that gave it a reputation for hospitality, which is as valid as ever, and enabled the town to support fifteen inns and beerhouses at its peak.

The surrounding villages joined in the 'beer and beds' bonanza and the tiny village of Barkway boasted an impressive twenty hostelries. The local farms were hard pressed to provide enough barley to sustain the trade – it's not surprising, therefore that another nearby village is named Barley!

Information kindly provided by the Buntingford Town Centre Management Team

The Bull

Cottered (Map Ref: 163 G3)   English/British   Average Price: £21.00

The Bull Public House
Cottered
Nr. Buntingford
Tel: 01763 281243

*The Bull offers a wide
selection of quality food*

Opening hours

M-F	12.00-3.00	6.30-11.00
Sat	12.00-3.00	6.30-11.00
Sun	12.00-3.00	7.00-10.30

Food served

M-F	12.00-2.00	6.30-9.30
	No food Tues evening	
Sat	12.00-2.00	6.30-9.30
Sun	12.00-2.00	7.00-9.00

Food style
English/British

Features & facilities
Child friendly (Over 7 yrs)
Disabled facilities
Garden/outside eating area
Real ales
Special diets catered for
Wheelchair access

The Bull is very popular with locals and visitors to the area. It is the sister pub of the Jolly Wagonners in Ardeley.

It has been run by Thomas Burley and Neil Martin for over nine years and has built a reputation for its friendly atmosphere, good food and good service.

Lunch and dinner is served every day, except on Tuesday evening and is available in both bars.

The Bull offers a wide selection of traditional, fresh, homemade food. The specials board changes regularly but firm favourites are the sausage and mash; steak, stilton and Guiness pie; sirloin of beef with a smoked bacon and cheese sauce; fresh crab; fillet of salmon and many more. The portions are generous and the staff always friendly and attentive.

The Bull is an attractive traditional English country pub with two open fires and stripped wooden floors. Most tables have a window position and there is a garden at the rear of the property. There are also two car parks.

The Sword in Hand

(English/British) (Average Price: £17.00) **Westmill** (Map Ref: **163** G3)

Westmill
Nr Buntingford SG9 9LQ
Tel: 01763 271356

*A delightful country pub
serving wonderful home
cooked food to the
highest standards*

Opening hours
Mon Closed
Tu-F 12.00-2.30 6.00-11.00
Sat 12.00-2.30 6.00-11.00
Sun 12.00noon - 10.00pm

Food served
Mon Closed
Tu-F 12.00-2.00 7.00-9.30
Sat 12.00-2.00 7.00-9.30
Sun 12.00noon - 8.00pm

Food style
English/British

Features & facilities
Child friendly
- High chairs
- Children's menu
Garden/Outside eating area
Non-smoking area
Private functions
Real ales
Special diets catered for
Vegetarian dishes
Wheelchair access
Wines - extensive selection

Heather Hoppleton has owned and run this successful and popular pub for the last 15 years.

The main part of the building dates back 500 years and was once the home of a noble Scottish family. Following a fire six years ago much of the building had to be re-built but many of the old timbers were salvaged and now you would never know that it wasn't all original. Outside is a delightful patio and garden with comfortable seating and wysteria covered pergola.

The food style is generally British but with a few continental twists and embellishments all lovingly created and prepared by chef Peter Moore.

Local produce is used wherever possible with fresh deliveries of meat, fish and vegetables every day from local suppliers. Favourites from the menu include swordfish with sweet pepper and olive butter; chicken breast stuffed with brie and wrapped in bacon; red pepper stuffed with herbs and rice and topped with cheese; fillet steak with melted stilton and, if you have room, try the banana and chocolate crumble.

REDEMPTION
SIGNATURE

10% Discount (FOOD ONLY)
Mon-Thurs all day

See terms & conditions on page 7. Expiry date: 31 December 2004

The Black Horse

Brent Pelham (Map Ref: **163** H3) (English/British) (Average Price: £20.00)

Pump Hill
Brent Pelham
Nr Buntingford SG9 0AP
Tel: 01279 777305

*A reputation for good
food, good service and a
friendly atmosphere*

Opening hours

M-F 12.00noon - 11.00pm
Sat 12.00noon - 11.00pm
Sun 12.00noon - 10.30pm

Food served

Mon 12.00-2.30 no food
Tu-Fr 12.00-2.30 7.00-9.30
Sat 12.00-2.30 7.00-9.30
Sun 12.00-5.00 no food

Food style
English/British

Features & facilities
Child friendly
 - Children's menu
Disabled facilities
Garden/Outside eating area
Non-smoking area
Private functions
Real ales
Vegetarian dishes
Wheelchair access

Brent Pelham is a small, rural village and is well served by this lovely country pub.

The mustard yellow façade and bright hanging baskets give you a warm, welcoming feeling as you approach. The inside is cosy with low ceilings and exposed beams that are decorated with a selection of brass and copper ornaments.

Since proprietors Frank and Paula took over 18 months ago their reputation for good food, good service and a friendly atmosphere has spread.

This is a family friendly establishment: children are welcome and the gardens are great for them to explore.

The separate restaurant is totally non-smoking and serves a good selection of traditional British cuisine. It can be hired for larger parties and special occasions.

Sunday lunch is very popular. A full roast with three courses for just £14.95 is excellent value, although due to its growing popularity booking is advisable.

Bed and breakfast is also offered.

Bushey

Bushey and Bushey Heath once formed an idyllic country village with a charming duckpond and a heath and commanded breathtaking views over the London landscape to the south. Now, largely subsumed by the growth of Watford, much of the heath is no more and Bushey is probably best known these days as the childhood home of popstar George Michael!

That's not to say, though, that it's not of historical or current interest. Bushey's rich history goes beyond even the Iron Age to an original Palaeolithic settlement. Mentioned in the Domesday Book as Bissei, part of the estate of the Norman Lord of the Manor Geoffrey de Mandeville, Bushey remained a quiet hamlet until the establishment of the Watford and Stanmore breweries and silk mills, in addition to the brick and rail industries fuelled expansion.

Strangely though, it is the arts that were to shape the village's future. The reason, quite literally, was in the water. Bushey, in the 18th and 19th centuries, was said to have the best water in the outskirts of North London and some London families sent their children to the village to avoid the city's cholera and typhoid epidemics.

Among the newcomers was Dr Thomas Monro, a physician to George III, who, as a patron of the arts, introduced many watercolorists to the area. Their works remain at the Bushey Museum as a record of Bushey life in the 19th century.

Many of their art studios survive too, as do the pond and the 13th century church of St James in the conservation area which covers the main part of the village.

The Mark Restaurant

Bushey Heath (Map Ref: 165 D7)   (International)   (Average Price: £18.00)

The Three Crowns Pub
1 High Road
Bushey Heath WD23 1EA
Tel: 020 8950 2851
Fax: 020 8421 8336

*The new menu is created
from a compilation of
international cuisines*

Opening hours
M-F   11.00am - 11.00pm
Sat   11.00am - 11.00pm
Sun   12.00noon - 10.30pm

Food served
Mon 12.00-2.30 Closed even.
Tu-Fr 12.00-2.30 7.00-10.00
Sat   12.00-2.30 7.00-10.00
Sun   12.00-3.00 6.30-9.00

Food style
International

Features & facilities
Child friendly
 - High chairs
Garden/Outside eating area
Non-smoking area
Real ales
Wines - extensive selection

Set in a listed building on Bushey High Road, right opposite the junction of Elstree Road, the building has been a pub since the 18th century.

It has been under new ownership and management for the last 15 months which has brought a number of changes. The new menu is created from a compilation of international cuisines but many British dishes such as beef, Guiness and mushroom pie; shank of lamb or a wonderful steak are still firm favourites.

You can choose to dine in the original pub and bar area with exposed beams, log fires and solid wood tables or in the new contemporary restaurant overlooking the garden.

Both the pub and restaurant are busy at weekends so it is advisable to book.

The service is friendly and the atmosphere relaxed.

REDEMPTION
SIGNATURE

Free bottle wine with a 2 course meal for a table of 2 or more, Tues-Fri evening

Voucher

See terms & conditions on page 7. Expiry date: 31 December 2004

Blue Check

(Continental)   (Average Price: £25.00)

144-146 High Street
Bushey WD23 3DH
Tel: 020 8421 8811

*This new restaurant is
chic, stylish and very
friendly*

Opening hours

M-F	12.00-3.00 6.00-12.00
Sat	Closed lunch 6.00-12.00
Sun	Reserved for private functions

Food style
Continental

Features & facilities
Child friendly
 - High chairs
 - Children's menu
Disabled facilities
Private functions
Special diets catered for
Vegetarian dishes
Wheelchair access

This new restaurant is chic, stylish and very friendly. You can choose where you would like to sit instead of being ushered to a table – an example of the friendly style of service that Blue Check is becoming renowned for.

The continental menu is varied with an excellent selection of meat, fish and vegetarian dishes and with quirky titles such as '52nd street' for medallions of beef, or 'ugly duckling' for breast of chicken, it will take you some time to choose. The chef draws experience from around the world using only the finest and freshest ingredients.

This is a great venue for private functions or business lunches as Blue Check has experience in catering for large numbers. Entertainment is a regular feature. Thursday night is Sinatra night and there is always live music on a Friday. The restaurant is often reserved on Sundays for private functions.

Manager David Johal runs a fine example of a first-class restaurant based around a formula of customer service and quality food.

REDEMPTION
SIGNATURE

25% Discount (FOOD ONLY)
Monday-Friday

See terms & conditions on page 7. Expiry date: 31 December 2004

41

St James

Bushey (Map Ref: 165 D7) (English/British) (Average Price: £35.00)

30 High Street
Bushey WD23 3HL
Tel: 020 8950 2480
Fax: 020 8950 4107

*English cuisine at its
very best*

Opening hours

M-F   12.00-3.00 6.30-9.30
Sat   12.00-3.00 6.30-9.30
Sun   Closed

Food style
English

Features & facilities
Disabled facilities
Non-smoking area
Private functions
Vegetarian dishes
Wheelchair access
Wines - extensive selection

Opened at the beginning of June 1997 this delightful restaurant is a surprise find in the heart of Bushey High Street. The menu blends flavours and contrasts and offers the very best in modern English cuisine.

Whilst traditionally English, influences have been incorporated from across Europe – especially France and Italy. Only the finest ingredients are used and the comprehensive menu changes with the seasons. Favourite dishes include chicken liver paté with toasted brioche and red onion gravy; roast rump of lamb with potato and onion cake, sauteé spinach, roast plum tomatoes and a basil jus and to complete the meal a chocolate marquise with white chocolate ice cream and coffee sauce.

Vegetarians are well catered for with a separate menu.

The stylish interior of the restaurant complements the cuisine with stripped wooden floors, exposed brickwork and brightly coloured walls.

If you appreciate good food and wine and want to try a London-style restaurant without travelling into London then St James is the place for you.

St James

Chinese **Average Price: £18.00**

144-146 High Street
Bushey Heath WD23 1EE
Tel: 020 8950 4886
Fax: 020 8950 9948

*A mix of Cantonese and
Thai cuisine, always
beautifully presented*

Opening hours

M-Th 12.00-2.00   6.00-11.00
Fr-Sa 12.00-2.00   6.00-11.30
Sun   12.00noon - 11.00pm

Food style
Chinese and Thai

Features & facilities
Child friendly
 - High chairs
Garden/Outside eating area
Non-smoking area
Vegetarian dishes

This new restaurant opened in December 2002
and is already proving to be very popular. The
smart decor is finished with a range of traditional
oriental ornaments and pictures.

The New China Restaurant serves a mix of
Cantonese and Thai cuisine, always beautifully
presented.

Popular dishes include the green curry or pad Thai
hat noodles which the chef highly recommends.
At lunchtime the Dim Sum is great for a quick
meal.

Ho-fun flat noodles are especially popular and
are cooked to your liking with a range of sauces
such as chicken and black bean.

On Sundays there is a special buffet served from
noon until 10.00pm. For £9.00 per person you can
help yourself to a selection of starters, crispy
aromatic duck, soup, main dishes and desserts.

There is a reasonable wine list and a range of
beers including Tsing Tao, Singaporean Tiger and
Thai Single beer.

REDEMPTION
SIGNATURE

10% Discount Mon-Fri

Except Chinese New Year, and from 14th Dec-4th Jan.

See terms & conditions on page 7. Expiry date: 31 December 2004

43

Harpenden

Is Harpenden a town or a village? This is a question that many visitors ask when they come across the genteel clutch of buildings and the immaculately maintained greens on either side of the High Street that the locals still refer to as 'the village'.

Yet Harpenden has been a town for more than a hundred years, complete with excellent shopping facilities, new housing and a wealth of leisure amenities such as the newly refurbished Harpenden Leisure Centre, which has a state-of-the-art swimming complex.

Thanks to a consistently thoughtful planning policy and its picturesque site on a dip-slope of the Chiltern Hills, the town retains a charm that's redolent of another era. A prime example is the Harpenden Railway Museum which nestles in a 'Harpenden-in-Bloom' prize-winning garden where working vintage signals, signposts and notice boards seem to grow out of the luxuriant shrubbery and blooms.

All this is overlooked by the 238 acre common, which climbs the hill to the south to a height of more than 400 feet above sea level and is mostly stewarded by the Town Council which jealously protects the public's right to enjoy 'air and exercise'. Today that includes everything from football to golf, cricket and art exhibitions, the annual 'Statty' fair and non-animal circuses.

Information kindly provided by the Harpenden Town Council

The Gibraltar Castle

(English/British) (Average Price: £20.00)

70 Lower Luton Road
Harpenden AL5 5AH
Tel: 01582 460005

Customers travel from miles around to sample the food

Opening hours

M-F 11.30-3.00 5.00-11.00
Sat 11.30am - 11.00pm
Sun 12.00noon - 10.30pm

Food served

M-Th 12.00-2.00 6.00-9.00
Sat 12.00-2.00 6.00-9.00
Sun 12.00-4.00

Booking is highly recommended

Food style
English/British

Features & facilities
Child friendly
Garden/Outside eating area
Real ales
Special diets catered for
Wines - extensive selection

This delightful, traditional English country pub is thought to be at least 350 years old. With its exposed beams, wooden floors and an open fireplace that is ideal for those cold winter days, and in contrast for the summer there is a stunning patio area where you can enjoy eating al fresco.

Proprietors Hamish and Sally Miller have built a reputation for the quality of the food and customers travel from miles around. The pub specialises in fish and seafood, fresh from the market. Unusual varieties such as monkfish, red snapper and marlin are popular choices when in season.

A range of smoked fish, sourced from one of the finest smokeries in western Scotland is also on offer. There is a varied menu including excellent Scottish fillet steaks, chicken with brie and Italian ham and imaginative salads.

All the food is freshly prepared, often using unique recipes and only the finest ingredients.

REDEMPTION
SIGNATURE

10% Discount (FOOD ONLY)
Monday-Wednesday Lunchtime

See terms & conditions on page 7. Expiry date: 31 December 2004

The Bean Tree

Harpenden (Map Ref: 165 D5)

(French)   (Average Price: £35.00)

20A Leyton Road
Harpenden AL5 2HU
Tel: 01582 460901
Fax: 01582 460826
enquiries@thebeantree.com
www.thebeantree.com

The dedicated team of chefs are passionate about the quality and freshness of the ingredients

Opening hours

Tu-F   12.00-2.00 (Last orders)
7.00-9.30 (Last orders)
Sat   Closed lunchtime
7.00-9.30 (Last orders)
Sun   12.30-2.30 (Last orders)

Food style
French

Features & facilities
Disabled facilities
Garden/Outside eating area
Non-smoking only
Special diets catered for
Vegetarian dishes
Wheelchair access
Wines - extensive selection

Set cosily in a converted cottage in the heart of Harpenden, The Bean Tree offers those who enjoy great food and wine, a destination restaurant to visit again and again. The ambience is calm and relaxed with a stylish modern slant. There is a lovely walled courtyard sheltered by an Indian bean tree - hence the name - where diners can relax in the warmer months.

The menu is French and the dedicated team of chefs are passionate about the quality and freshness of the ingredients, and great care is taken to source quality ingredients.

The seasonally-changing menu includes dishes such as a starter of seared scallops, fine beans and trompette de mort casserole with paprika butter sauce; a main course of shelled lobster, broad bean galette with a brown shrimp and crab dressing and a dessert of ginger crème brulée with cherry compote. The superb wine list fully complements the great food. As you would expect, French wines are given centre stage in the list with Burgundy red and whites leading the way.

REDEMPTION
SIGNATURE

£10 discount from wine choice
Lunch Tues-Fri and Dinner Tue-Thurs
See terms & conditions on page 7. Expiry date: 31 December 2004

New Taj Mahal

Harpenden (Map Ref: 165 D5)

12 Station Road,
Harpenden AL5 4SE
Tel: 01582 764188
       01582 715280

Customers travel from all over the county to experience the fabulous cuisine

Opening hours

M-F	12.00-2.30	6.00-11.30
Sat	12.00-2.30	6.00-11.30
Sun	12.00-2.30	6.00-11.30

Food style
Indian

Features & facilities
Child friendly
 - Children's menu
Disabled facilities
Private functions
Special diets catered for
Vegetarian dishes
Wheelchair access
Wines - extensive selection

The New Taj Mahal which opened 25 years ago was the first Indian restaurant in Harpenden. Since then it has been owned and successfully run by Mr Khan and his experienced team.

You are always assured of a warm welcome, indeed the restaurant was awarded a Master Chef five star award for its food and service. It has a strong local following and many customers travel from all over the county to experience the restaurant's fabulous cuisine.

The freshly prepared dishes are influenced by regional cuisine from all parts of India. Kormas and baltis are always very popular. However, the chef's specials are definitely not to be overlooked. Try, for example, the mild nowabi murghi stick. This is a superb eastern dish of tender spices with chicken in a highly flavoured sauce and is highly acclaimed locally.

The New Taj Mahal also has a good selection of vegetarian dishes, can cater for special dietary requirements and has a separate children's menu, so everyone is well catered for.

REDEMPTION
SIGNATURE

Buy one main meal and get one FREE, Sunday-Thursday

See terms & conditions on page 7. Expiry date: 31 December 2004

The Old Bell

Harpenden (Map Ref: **165** D5)   (English/British)   (Average Price: £20.00)

177 Luton Road
Harpenden AL5 3BN
Tel: 01582 712484
Fax: 01582 715015

This delightful country pub is an oasis from the hustle and bustle of daily life

Opening hours

M-F	11.00am - 11.00pm
Sat	11.00am - 11.00pm
Sun	12.00noon - 10.30pm

Food served

M-F	11.00am - 10.00pm
Sat	11.00am - 10.00pm
Sun	12.00noon - 9.00pm

Food style

English/British, specialising in fish

Features & facilities

Disabled facilities
Garden/Outside eating area
Non-smoking area
Real ales
Vegetarian dishes
Wines - extensive selection

Back in 1735, The Old Bell was part of a farm known as the 'Old Bell Ground'. By 1835 the building had been transformed into a beer house and became a fully fledged licensed public house in 1873.

This delightful country pub is an oasis from the hustle and bustle of daily life. The atmosphere is warm, homely and very relaxing with its traditional oak beamed interior, hanging baskets and smart garden.

The food is the epitome of the best of modern British pubs. An exhaustive selection of meat, fish and vegetarian dishes are displayed on blackboards around the bar and restaurant. Everything is freshly cooked, using only the best ingredients and the portions are generous.

Fish is the house speciality but whatever you choose the same commitment and enthusiasm will be put into creating the perfect dish.

The staff are friendly and help to enhance the 'home from home' atmosphere. There's no rush, so you can relax and enjoy a leisurely meal or pop in for a snack any time of the day.

Part of the Chef and Brewer chain, it has a well deserved reputation for quality food, fine wines and real ales.

Nicholls Brasserie

(Modern European) (Average Price: £21.50)

61 High Street
Harpenden AL5 2SL
Tel: 01582 462555
Fax: 01582 462556
www.nichollsonline.com

A warm and comfortable
atmosphere - fresh fish
dishes are a speciality

Opening hours

M-F 10.30-2.30 (last orders)
6.30-10.00 (last orders)
Sat 10.30-10.00 (last orders)
Sun 10.30-8.30 (last orders)

Food style
Modern European

Features & facilities
Air conditioned
Child friendly
 - High chairs
Live jazz on Sundays
Non-smoking area
Vegetarian dishes
Wines - extensive selection

Nicholls Brasserie opened in 1998 on the historic High Street in Harpenden. The Nicholl's team restored the building renovating the interior to create a warm, comfortable atmosphere, in their unique signature colours.

Within days, word had spread about their food - especially the superb 'Sea Blackboard'. Fish is a speciality with fresh deliveries daily.

It is open every day from 10.30, serving English breakfasts alongside fresh handmade coffee and croissants.

In addition to the main menu, there is a superb 3-course lunch, and for those who prefer it, a lighter choice. The fresh fish boards offer a wide choice ranging from whole seabass to red snapper, shark and tuna steaks, fresh salmon, cod and halibut. Shellfish is always available with dishes such as king prawns with the chef's butter of the day or mussels in white wine, garlic and chilli.

Sundays cannot be beaten with the infamous Nicholls All Day Brunch served until 8.30pm. Enjoy a late breakfast or a relaxed Sunday lunch with your family.

Booking is advisable at the weekend. Other Nicholls Brasseries can be found in Bedford, Berkhamsted and in Woburn.

Royal Orchid

Harpenden (Map Ref: **165** D5)   Thai   Average Price: £15.00

41 High Street
Harpenden
Tel: 01582 761807

*Serves a delightful mix
of traditional Thai
cuisine*

Opening hours

M-F	12.00-2.00	6.00-11.00
Sat	12.00-2.00	6.00-11.00
Sun	12.00-2.00	6.00-11.00

Food served

M-F	12.00-2.00	6.00-10.45
Sat	12.00-2.00	6.00-10.45
Sun	12.00-2.00	6.00-10.45

Food style
Thai

Features & facilities
Child friendly
- High chairs
Non-smoking area
Private functions
Special diets catered for
Vegetarian dishes
Wines - extensive selection

The restaurant is split over two floors with four individual rooms, making it ideal for small parties of up to 25 people or intimate dinners.

Set in a listed building, the large attractive panelled window to the front gives the restaurant a light and airy feel. Inside, it is pleasantly decorated with comfortable rush backed seating.

The Royal Orchid has been established for just over 4 years and serves a delightful mix of traditional Thai cuisine, all cooked from fresh ingredients on the premises. Favourite dishes include the green curries, or the crispy beef with chilli and basil. The chef's special menu changes regularly to reflect changes in tastes and seasons.

The wine list offers a good selection of wines from around the world, all reasonably priced.

All the staff are very friendly and helpful and offer efficient but unhurried service.

REDEMPTION
SIGNATURE

10% Discount
Sunday-Thursday

See terms & conditions on page 7. Expiry date: 31 December 2004

Hatfield

including Brookmans Park and Essendon

Hatfield Highlights

- Hatfield House

- The Old Palace

- The Galleria Shopping Centre and cinema complex

- Roe Hill Hall Playing Fields and Multi-Use Sports Area

The town is probably most famous for the historic Jacobean Hatfield House where Princess Elizabeth Tudor was confined before learning in 1558 that she had become Queen.

Home to the Cecil family for 400 years, the house is open to the public for Elizabethan banquets and a host of other events but visitors are also free to visit the exquisite organic gardens, nature trails, gift and garden shops, licensed restaurant and the national collection of model soldiers.

More recently, Hatfield made its mark as a centre of excellence in the aviation industry and as the birthplace of such legendary pioneering planes such as the Mosquito, Comet and Trident. The opening of the de Havilland aircraft factory triggered the town's economic and population boom just before the Second World War and de Havilland, later Hawker Siddley and finally British Aerospace, rapidly became the district's largest employers.

The old town is traditionally linked with transport – its growth was fuelled by trade from the Great North Road and later the railways - so aviation was the logical next step. It brought new prosperity with which to shape the new town around the old, creating today's pleasant, spacious, tree-lined environment in which the high tech Hatfield Business Park and University of Hertfordshire have grown and continue to thrive.

With a 22 minute commuter rail service direct to London King's Cross and the A1(M) and M25 just a few miles away and with rapid road access to London, Hatfield's unusually well-connected.

Information kindly supplied by Hatfield Town Council

Rose & Crown

Essendon (Map Ref: **165** F5)

(English/British) (Average Price: £21.00)

High Road
Essendon
Hatfield
Tel: 01707 261229

Justifiably proud of a reputation for top quality food, served in a stylish and relaxed envirnoment

Opening hours

M-F	11.30-3.00	5.30-11.00
Sat	11.30-4.00	6.00-11.00
Sun	12.00-4.00	7.00-10.30

Food served

Mon	12.00-2.00	
Tu-Fr	12.00-2.00	7.00-9.00
Sat	12.00-2.00	7.00-9.00
Sun	12.00-2.00	

Food style
Modern English/British

Features & facilities
Child friendly
Garden/Outside eating area
Non-smoking area
Private functions
Real ales
Special diets catered for
Vegetarian dishes
Wheelchair access
Wines - extensive selection

Set in the small village of Essendon, this delightful country pub has a weatherboarded façade, hanging baskets and neat gardens at the rear.

The Davis family are justifiably proud of the restaurant's excellent reputation and always offer a warm welcome to regular and new customers alike. The light and airy restaurant has recently been refurbished and offers a blend of contemporary and classic furnishings in a relaxed and stylish environment.

The Rose & Crown offers excellent value for money and top quality modern British cuisine. Everything is freshly cooked to order, using only the finest ingredients, most of which are sourced locally. The pan fried scallops are a real treat.

The food is complemented by an extensive wine list and a selection of ten malt whiskies.

Snacks and food are served either in the comfortable bar or outside in the garden.

REDEMPTION
SIGNATURE

10% Discount (FOOD ONLY)
Monday-Thursday

See terms & conditions on page 7. Expiry date: 31 December 2004

Methi Indian Cuisine

Indian · Average Price: £15.00

Brookmans Park (Map Ref: 165 F6)

81-82 Bradmore Green
Brookmans Park
Hatfield AL9 7QT
Tel: 01707 662233 / 655200

A wide range of freshly prepared dishes served in a contemporary restaurant

Opening hours
M-F   5.30 to late
Sat   5.30 to late
Sun   5.30 to late

Food style
Indian

Features & facilities
Child friendly
- High chairs
- Children's menu
Disabled facilities
Private functions
Vegetarian dishes
Wheelchair access
Wines - extensive selection

Methi only opened in October 2002 but has already achieved an excellent local reputation and is well worth a visit.

The restaurant has a contemporary feel, with well spaced tables, comfortable seating and a warm and friendly atmosphere.

It offers a wide range of freshly prepared dishes ranging from old favourites such as baltis and kormas, to the locally renowned Methi Raja which is chicken or lamb prepared with strips of green peppers, onions, methi and a selection of Tandoori spices, drowned in red wine and served with rice and puffed parata. Vegetarians are well catered for.

On Wednesday nights a banquet evening is held when diners can sample superb dishes from a wide and varying selection. The restaurant can cater for large parties.

Don't forget to book at weekends as it's always busy!

REDEMPTION
SIGNATURE

Free bottle of house wine
for tables of 4 or more, any day except Wednesday

See terms & conditions on page 7. Expiry date: 31 December 2004

53

Gobions Restaurant, Brookmans Park Hotel

Brookmans Park (Map Ref: 165 F6) (English/British) (Average Price: £14.95)

Bradmore Green
Brookmans Park, Hatfield
AL9 7QW
Tel: 01707 653577
Fax: 01707 661527
www.thebrookmansparkhotel.co.uk

*Monday night is
buffet night*

Opening hours

M-F	11.00-3.00	5.30-11.00
Sat	11.00am	- 11.00pm
Sun	12.00noon	- 10.30pm

Food served

M-Th	12.00-2.30	7.00-9.00
F-Sat	12.00-2.30	7.00-9.30
Sun	12.00-3.00	Closed

Food style
English/British

Features & facilities
Disabled facilities
Garden/patio area
Non-smoking restaurant
Real ales
Special diets catered for
Vegetarian dishes
Weddings/Private functions
Wheelchair access
Wines - extensive selection

This small, privately run hotel is set in the heart of the charming village of Brookmans Park. The hotel has been part of the local community for over 50 years but under new ownership for the last year has seen recent improvements.

The Gobions Restaurant is open for lunch and dinner with a lunchtime special of traditional home cooked dishes such as steak and kidney pie or toad in the hole. Bar snacks are also available.

In the evening the table d'hôte menu changes regularly offering a choice of around six starters and eight main courses. There are also chef's specials on offer with popular dishes like red snapper or rack of lamb. All dishes are freshly cooked and the chef prides himself on the flavours he creates with his home-made sauces.

The hotel also offers facilities for small business meetings or conferences and has six letting bedrooms.

54

Hemel Hempstead

including the villages of Bovingdon and Flaunden

Hemel Hempstead Highlights

- St Mary's Church

- The Old Town Hall Arts Centre

- Gadebridge Park

For further information about this town, Berkhamsted, Tring and surrouding villages contact:

Dacorum Information Centre
Marlowes
Hemel Hempstead HP1 1DT
Tel: 01442 234222
Fax: 01442 230427
www.dacorum.gov.uk
informationcentre@dacorum.gov.uk

Opening hours:
Mon-Fri 9.30am - 5.00pm
Sat   9.30am - 1.00pm
Closed Sundays and Bank Holidays

Information kindly supplied by Dacorum Information Centre

Hemel Hempstead is really two towns, sharing a name but each with its own distinct personality.

The old town, whose High Street was described by Sir John Betjeman as 'one of the most agreeable streets in Hertfordshire' clings to the historic, mainly Norman St Mary's church at its centre, parts of which dates from around 1150 AD. The variegated mix of architectural styles from Tudor to Georgian, Victorian and modern and many listed buildings creates a town full of character that's a delight to explore.

With a vast range of eateries from the traditional English inn to Italian, Indian and Thai cuisine, the High Street caters for the most cosmopolitan of tastes – as does the Old Town Hall Arts Centre with its packed programme of music, comedy, drama and local and national exhibitions.

The new town of Hemel Hempstead was among the first to be built after the Second World War and it added a host of modern amenities to the old town's character to create the best of both worlds.

Now home to more than eighty thousand people, this vibrant town features an extensive indoor shopping centre, the Marlowes pedestrian area, and the bustling traditional open-air market – as well as local shops, pubs and community centres, providing a focal point in each of the town's residential neighbourhoods.

With easy train services south to London Euston and north to Milton Keynes, Birmingham, Manchester, Liverpool and Scotland, plus excellent road links via the M1, M10 and M25, Hemel Hempstead is one of the best-connected towns in the county.

Cochin South Indian Coastal Cuisine

Hemel Hempstead (Map Ref: 165 D6)   (Indian)   (Average Price: £13.50)

61 High Street
Hemel Hempstead Old Town
HP1 3AF
Tel: 01442 233777
Fax: 01442 231777
info@cochincuisine.co.uk

Hertfordshire Food &
Wine Award 2002 winner
for best vegetarian and
seafood selection

Opening hours

M-Th 12.00-2.30 6.00-11.00
Fri   12.00-2.30 5.30-11.30
Sat   12.00-2.30 5.30-11.30
Sun   12.00-2.30 6.00-11.00

Food style
South Indian coastal cuisine

Features & facilities
Private functions
Vegetarian dishes

The independently owned Cochin restaurant is the first in Hertfordshire to specialise in southern Indian coastal cuisine.

Located in the Old Town of Hemel Hempstead, this is a stylish restaurant with comfortable and spacious seating. The contemporary design blends well with some traditional wall hangings and ornate south Indian lamps.

The traditional dishes from the Kerala region of southern India are freshly prepared by expert chef Narayanan Karolil.

This style of cuisine is very different from other regions of India – deep sea fish, shellfish, luscious fruits and vegetables combined with a unique mix of aromatic herbs and spices. Try the amazing mango and banana curry - one of the most popular dishes from Kerala.

The atmosphere is enhanced by the soft traditional music which transports you to Kerala, one of the most beautiful places in the world.

The fully air conditioned restaurant is split over two levels so it can accomodate small parties and private functions. Its reputation is expanding so book early - it's well worth a visit and very reasonably priced.

South India's Coastal Cuisine

Bobsleigh Grill, Rotisserie, Bar

(English/British)   (Average Price: £20.00)   **Bovingdon** (Map Ref: **164** C6)

Bobsleigh Hotel
Hempstead Road, Bovingdon
Hemel Hempstead HP3 0DS
Tel: 01442 833276
Fax: 01442 836791
bobsleigh@macdonald-hotels.co.uk

*The food is in a
steakhouse brasserie
style*

Opening hours
M-Sat 6.00pm - 9.30pm
Sun   12.00noon - 3.00pm

Food style
English/British

Features & facilities
Child friendly
- High chairs
- Children's menu
Garden/Outside eating area
Non-smoking restaurant
Special diets catered for
Vegetarian dishes
Weddings/Private functions
Wheelchair access
Wines - extensive selection

A fine example of old world hospitality meeting new world facilities.

The restaurant has recently been completely refurbished in a much more modern and contemporary style with spacious, comfortable seating and wooden floors.

The food is steakhouse brasserie in style with a good selection of freshly prepared meat and fish dishes. There is an excellent mixture of French and new world wines to complement your meal. The whole restaurant is non-smoking.

Before, or after dinner, you can relax and enjoy a drink or cocktail in the Acacia Bar, the ideal place to unwind after a busy day.

The hotel also offers 47 bedrooms, all ensuite, with a range of conference and banqueting facilities.

REDEMPTION
SIGNATURE

10% discount (FOOD ONLY)
any time, any day

See terms & conditions on page 7. Expiry date: 31 December 2004

57

Casanova Ristorante Italiano

Hemel Hempstead (Map Ref: 165 D6) (Italian) (Average Price: £20.00)

75 Waterhouse Street
Hemel Hempstead HP1 1ED
Tel: 01442 247482

*A quality Italian
restaurant with an
extensive menu*

Opening hours

M-F	12.00-2.00	6.45-11.00
Sat	Closed	6.45-11.00
Sun	Closed	

Food style
Italian

Features & facilities
Child friendly
- High chairs
Non-smoking area
Private functions including
  hen nights and birthday
  parties
Wheelchair access
Wines - extensive selection

Giancarlo Benigno, Carlo to his friends and clients, celebrated 25 years of running this delightful Italian restaurant in 2003. Over these years the restaurant has grown in popularity with local people and now has a loyal and devoted following.

The menu is extensive and focuses on traditional Italian dishes as well as some other favourites from around the world.

Some of the favourite dishes include penne carbonara; veal ninfetta; pollo al dolcelatte; gamberoni al burro e aglio and you have to try the homemade tiramisu, it's delicious!

Occasionally, during the week there are theme nights, for example 60s nights and Roman evenings, which have always been a great success.

The food is complemented by a reasonably priced wine list with a generous selection of Italian wines and a well stocked bar.

25 years is a long time to run a restaurant and the many loyal clients bear testimony to the continued popularity of this establishment.

Well worth a visit!

Green Dragon

Flaunden (Map Ref: **164** C6)

Flaunden
Hemel Hempstead HP3 0PP
Tel: 01442 832269

*Traditional English
menu of home cooked
food*

Opening hours

M-F 11.00-3.00 5.30-11.00
Sat 11.00am - 11.00pm
Sun 12.00noon - 10.30pm

Food served

M-F 12.00-2.00 7.00-9.30
Sat 12.00-2.00 7.00-9.30
Sun 12.00-2.00

Food style
English/British

Features & facilities
Child friendly
 - Children's menu
Garden/Outside eating area
Non-smoking area
Private functions
Real ales
Special diets catered for
Vegetarian dishes
Wheelchair access
Wines - extensive selection

A delightful English country pub set in the rural village of Flaunden. The surrounding countryside is beautiful and very popular with walkers, cyclists and anyone who enjoys a drive in the country.

The cosy bar has exposed beams, a real fire and comfortable furnishings. There is a friendly and relaxed atmosphere so you will soon feel like a local.

Landlady Denise Hope has twenty years' experience in the trade and ensures that Green Dragon's traditional English menu offers home cooked food served in generous portions. The service is always friendly and relaxed.

There is also a small garden where you can enjoy the summer sunshine.

REDEMPTION
SIGNATURE

Free bottle of wine
with a 2 course meal, Mon-Thurs

See terms & conditions on page 7. Expiry date: 31 December 2004

Hertford

including the villages of Epping Green, Hertingfordbury, Little Berkhamsted, Newgate Street, Stapleford and Watton-at-Stone

Hertford Highlights

• Hertford Castle and grounds

• Hertford Museum

• St Leonards Church

• Castle Hall

For further information about the town and surrounding villages contact:

Hertford Town & Tourist
Information Centre
10 Market Place,
Hertford SG14 1DG
Tel: 01992 584322
Fax: 01992 534724
Email: hertford@eetb.info

Opening hours:
Mon-Fri 9.00am - 5.00pm
Sat   9.30am - 1.00pm
Closed Sundays and Bank Holidays

*Information kindly supplied by
Hertford Town & Tourist
Information Centre*

Strategically sited at the confluence of four rivers; the Mimram, Rib, Beane and the Lea, Hertford originally derived its importance as an inland port and thriving market town. Today, the county town blends the best of rural and urban lifestyles. It also combines its legacy of picturesquely ancient architecture and antiquities with a host of pubs, clubs, restaurants, chic continental-style pavement cafés and specialist shops from the ultra hip to the quaintly old-fashioned.

Hertford is steeped in history and there are plenty of monuments worth visiting, all within a few steps of the town's bustling centre, where you'll find the town's artefact packed museum.

Hertford Castle, parts of which date back to the 15th century, once formed part of London's outer ring of defence and, in 673 AD, was host to the first ever General Synod of the English Church. This may explain the proliferation of 'spike' style church towers to be found in and around the town and in nearby villages such as Much Hadham (the Bishops of London's country seat for 800 years), Benington and Ardeley.

Twenty minutes from Stansted Airport, Hertford is as well-connected as it's well-preserved, with its two rail stations providing a link to London in under an hour and major routes such as the M25, A1 (M), A10 and M11 within just a few minutes' drive.

Elbert Wurlings

(Modern European)   (Average Price: £25.00)   **Hertford** (Map Ref: **166** G5)

Pegs Lane
Hertford SG13 8EG
Tel: 01992 509153
Fax: 01992 509153
info@elberts.co.uk
www.elberts.co.uk

*"Discover a cocktail
heaven in Hertford"*

Opening hours

M-W 12.00-3.00 7.00-11.00
M-W 12.00-3.00 7.00-2.00am
Sat   7.00pm - 2.00am
Sun   12.00 - 6.00pm

Food served

W-F   12.00-3.00 7.00-10.00
Sat   7.00pm - 10.00pm
Sun   12.00 - 3.00pm

Food style
Modern European

Features & facilities
Child friendly
- High chairs
- Children's menu
Disabled facilities
Private functions
Special diets catered for
Vegetarian dishes
Wheelchair access
Wines - extensive selection

Elbert Wurlings is a first class multifunctional venue located two minutes' walk from Hertford's centre and consists of a restaurant, waitressed lounge and contemporary bar. Its interior is warm and inviting for its patrons who can relax and enjoy the distinct and elegantly designed rooms. Each area is designed to compliment the other.

Elbert Wurlings won the 'Best Interior Design', southern regional finals, Theme Awards in 2003 and was described by Bethan Ryder in Theme Magazine as "a cocktail heaven in Hertford".

The ground floor restaurant's à la carte menu offers a variety of modern European dishes created from the finest fresh local produce and designed to tempt you with uncompromising flavours and styles. The menu is changed every six weeks. There is also a daily lunchtime and evening specials menu for those is a hurry which is great value for money.

Live music is played in the lounge and ground floor bar, which when combined with the unparalleled food and cocktails, makes Elbert Wurlings the ideal place to entertain and be entertained.

Photos: Noel Critchley

Cafe Pasta

Hertford (Map Ref: 166 G5) (Italian) (Average Price: £14.00)

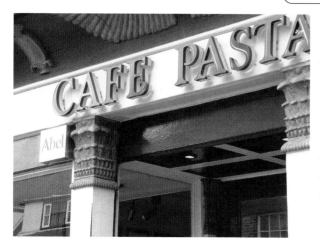

42 Fore Street
Hertford SG14 1BY
Tel: 01992 554624
Fax: 01992 554625
www.pizzaexpress.com

*Friendly Italian
restaurant with an
extensive menu*

Opening hours
M-F 11.30am - midnight
Sat 11.30am - midnight
Sun 12.00 noon - 11.30pm

Food served
M-F 12 noon - midnight
Sat 12 noon - midnight
Sun 12.00 noon-11.30pm

Food style
Italian

Features & facilities
Child friendly
- High chairs
Private functions
Special diets catered for
Vegetarian dishes
Wheelchair access
Wines - extensive selection

In 1999 Cafe Pasta opened in Hertford and has grown in popularity year-on-year, so booking is advisable at peak times.

The cheerful and attentive staff are always pleased to answer any questions you may have about the menu or weekly specials and the chef is always happy to accommodate special requests.

The restaurant is bright and airy and offers an extensive Italian menu ranging from delicious salads to pizzas, grills and of course, fantastic pasta dishes. The weekly specials board, with fresh, seasonal produce, enables the regular Cafe Pasta customer to try something new.

Whether you are looking for a venue for a private party or a business function, Cafe Pasta will cater for all your needs. The function room is free to hire for up to 40 people so it's definitely a place to add to your list.

The Stone House

7-11 Bull Plain
Hertford SG14 1DY
Tel: 01992 553736
Fax: 01992 534032
hertford@thestone-house.co.uk

*A stylish venue with an
emphasis on quality
across the board*

Opening hours

M-W 10.00am - 11.00pm
Thur 10.00am - 12.00am
Fri 10.00am - 1.00am
Sat 10.00am - 1.00am
Sun 10.00am - 10.30pm

Food served
Until one hour before
closing

Food style
English/British with a twist

Features & facilities
Disabled facilities
Garden/Outside eating area
Non-smoking area
Private functions
Vegetarian dishes
Wheelchair access

*Average price for main
meal only

The Stone House opened in December 2002 to fill the demand for a sophisticated but relaxed, high quality venue in Hertford.

The Stone House is something different - a stylish venue with the whole emphasis on good quality right across the board, from food and drink to entertainment, decor and furnishings and with a real focus on customer service.

It offers a warm welcome throughout the day or night where you can relax and chat to friends with a cappuccino or latte, meet for lunch, unwind with a drink after work, or eat, drink and party the night away.

Favourite dishes from the menu include The Stone House burger, sausage and mash – The Stone House style, topped spuds plus a range of quality salads and pastas.

The Stone House offers an innovative range of cocktails and shooters and their special milkshakes are pure liquid indulgence.

THE **stone** HOUSE

REDEMPTION
SIGNATURE

Free 175ml glass of house wine with
every main meal - all day, everyday

See terms & conditions on page 7. Expiry date: 31 December 2004

63

The Beehive

Epping Green (Map Ref: 165 F6)   (English/British)   (Average Price: £17.50)

Epping Green
Nr. Little Berkhamsted
Hertford SG13 8NB
Tel: 01707 875959

A picturesque public house serving quality ales and excellent food – specialising in fish

Opening hours

M-F	11.30-2.30	5.30-11.00
Sat	11.30-3.00	6.00-11.00
Sun	12.00-5.00	

Food served

M-F	12.00-2.00	7.00-9.00
Sat	12.00-2.30	7.00-9.00
Sun	12.00-4.00	

Food style
English/British, specialising in fish

Features & facilities
Garden/Outside eating area
Non-smoking area
Real ales
Vegetarian dishes
Wheelchair access
Wines - good selection

Husband and wife Maurice and Marie offer a friendly welcome and over the past 5 years have built a reputation for excellent food and very generous portions.

Specialising in fresh fish, the blackboard menu changes every day to offer the best from the market. Skate and crab are always popular choices. The menu also offers a varied selection of steaks, chicken and vegetarian dishes. If you're just after a quick bite, a full snack menu is available from the bar. The main eating area is now almost completely non-smoking.

The service is always friendly and efficient and the bar always offers a guest ale and a range of malt whiskies.

The woodburning stoves in the winter and the hanging baskets in the summer add to the ambience of this fine hostelry.

The pub is easy to find on the main road between Little Berkhamsted and Newgate Street and there is a large car park.

REDEMPTION
SIGNATURE

Free bottle of house wine
with a two course meal for table of 4, Mon-Thurs

See terms & conditions on page 7. Expiry date: 31 December 2004

All Seasons Restaurant

(English/British) (Average Price: £20.00) **Hertingfordbury** (Map Ref: 165 F5)

The White Horse Hotel
Hertingfordbury SG14 2LB
Tel: 01992 586791
Fax: 01992 550809
www.macdonald-hotels.co.uk

*The mix of old and new
creates an enchantingly
relaxed atmosphere
overlooking the grounds*

Opening hours
M-F 12.30-2.15 7.00-9.30
Sat Closed lunch 7.00-9.30
Sun 12.30-3.00 7.00-9.30

Food style
English/British but with
many French influences

Features & facilities
Garden/Outside eating area
Non smoking area
Real Ales
Special diets catered for
Weddings/Private functions

This is a contemporary restaurant set in a beautiful conservatory overlooking the gardens of this exquisite 400 year old country hotel.

French chef, William Morvan, provides a contemporary selection of dishes with a blend of traditional English and French dishes. Choose from either the à la carte or table d'hôte menus, both of which are prepared using fresh produce and cooked on the premises. The fine Scottish beef, is a real speciality.

The service is excellent - formal yet discreet – and the mix of old and new creates an enchantingly relaxed atmosphere overlooking the grounds.

Sunday lunch, with traditional English roasts, is delicious and at £7.95 is excellent value for money. Booking is advisable.

Weddings, family parties and business events are all expertly catered for. For a less formal meal, try the Mimrams Bar - see page 66 for details.

REDEMPTION
SIGNATURE

10% Discount
Any day.

See terms & conditions on page 7. Expiry date: 31 December 2004

Mimrams Bar

Hertingfordbury (Map Ref: 165 F5) (English/British) (Average Price: £14.00)

The White Horse Hotel
Hertingfordbury SG14 2LB
Tel: 01992 586791
Fax: 01992 550809
www.macdonald-hotels.co.uk

*All the food is freshly
cooked on the premises*

Opening hours

M-F	12.00-2.30	6.00-9.30
Sat	12.00-2.30	6.00-9.30
Sun	12.00-2.30	6.00-9.30

Food style
English/British

Features & facilities
Garden/Outside eating area
Real ales
Special diets catered for

Set in a wonderful 400 year old coaching inn this informal restaurant is comfortable, stylish and relaxed.

The ambience is enhanced by the exposed beams, tasteful decor and open log fires in the winter. In the summer months, enjoy the hotel's fantastic gardens.

The food is all freshly cooked on the premises. Traditional English fish and chips is a speciality or homemade chicken curry with all the trimmings is another of the restaurant's most popular dishes.

The Mimrams Bar offers a good selection of wines and real ales, all at a reasonable price.

Hertingfordbury is a lovely little village and ideally situated for exploring some of the treasures of the county. Hertford Castle, Hatfield House and Knebworth are all just a short drive away.

For a more formal occasion try the All Seasons Restaurant - see page 65 for details.

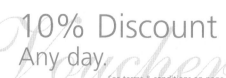

Caffé Uno

(Italian) (Average Price: £15.00)

Hertford (Map Ref: **166** G5)

21 Fore Street
Hertford SG14 1DH
Tel: 01992 504674
Fax: 01992 503031
www.caffeuno.co.uk

Warm and welcoming at any time of the day – all the food at Caffé Uno is cooked to order

Opening hours

M-F	10.00-11.00
Sat	10.00-11.30
Sun	11.00-10.30

Food served

M-F	12.00-11.00
Sat	10.00-11.30
Sun	11.00-10.30

Food style
Italian

Features & facilities
Child friendly
- High chairs
- Children's menu
Non-smoking area
Private functions
Special diets catered for
Vegetarian dishes

Caffé Uno in Hertford is a warm and friendly Italian restaurant conveniently located in the centre of town. With seating at tables for up to 35 it's a great place for parties.

All the food at Caffé Uno is cooked to order, from a great selection of grilled meat and fish dishes to tasty pasta dishes and delicious thin crust pizzas. The Italian chef also creates weekly blackboard specials and menus to suit requirements offering even more choice and variety for the loyal Caffé Uno regular.

Quality is a passion at Caffé Uno and you'll find that passion every day. It is open from breakfast 'til late seven days a week. Perfect for that morning cup of latte, ideal for lunch and great for dinner, it's the perfect place to go at any time. A warm welcome is guaranteed.

REDEMPTION
SIGNATURE

2 Free bottles of wine for tables of 6 or more

See terms & conditions on page 7. Expiry date: 31 December 2004

Publishers note: the photos depicted were not taken at the Hertford restaurant

Le Papillon

Stapleford (Map Ref: 162 F4) (English/British) (Average Price: £16.00)

Woodhall Arms
17 High Road
Stapleford, Hertford SG14 3NW
Tel: 01992 535123
Fax: 01992 582772
www.papillon-woodhallarms.co.uk

A very popular restaurant, consistently serving high standards of freshly cooked food with generous portions

Opening hours

M-F	12.00-2.00	6.30-10.30
Sat	12.00-2.00	6.30-10.30
Sun	12.00-2.30	6.30-9.30

Food style
English/British with other continental influences

Features & facilities
Bed & breakfast available
Child friendly
- Children's menu
- High chairs
Disabled facilities
Garden/Outside eating area
Non-smoking area
Real ales
Special diets catered for
Vegetarian dishes
Weddings/private functions
Wheelchair access
Wines - extensive selection

Please note the hotel and restaurant are currently being refurbished, due for completion in 2004

Le Papillon is a very popular restaurant which has built its reputation by consistently serving high standards of freshly cooked food with generous portions.

Inside, there are a choice of rooms in which to eat including the main bar area and a lovely conservatory with doors overlooking the patio and fields beyond. Parties and wedding receptions can all be catered for with personally chosen menus by arrangement.

The extensive menu has over a dozen starters, 26 main courses and 14 desserts to choose from. It also includes a generous selection of fresh fish dishes and three vegetarian options, so there is something for everyone.

Sample dishes from the menu include a starter of hot avocado with a delightful combination of fresh prawns, provençale sauce and glazed with a mild cheese fondu; followed by rack of prime English lamb served with a real ale and wild mushroom sauce and then finally crêpe jubilee, a freshly made sweet pancake filled with vanilla ice cream and finished with a hot black cherry and red wine sauce.

As you would expect for such a popular restaurant, you will need to book at the weekends and it is also very busy at other peak times.

Ponsbourne Park Hotel

Newgate Street Village
Hertford SG13 8QZ
Tel: 01707 876191
Fax: 01707 875190
ponsbournepark@lineone.net
www.ponsbournepark.co.uk

A blend of classic
elegance brought
up-to-date by a stylish
and creative design

Opening hours

M-F	12.00-3.00	6.30-10.00
Sat	12.00-3.00	6.30-10.00
Sun	12.00-3.00	6.30-10.00

Food style
International - a range of British and French cuisines

Features & facilities
Child friendly
Garden/Outside eating area
Non-smoking area
Special diets catered for
Vegetarian dishes
Weddings/Private functions
Wheelchair access
Wines - extensive selection

The Ponsbourne Park Hotel was built in 1876 as the home of William Carlisle who leased it to the Roman Catholic Church in 1932 as a convent school known as St. Dominic's. The main house, surrounded by 200 acres of countryside, offers a blend of classic elegance brought stunningly up-to-date by a stylish and creative design.

The restaurant offers a modern British and contemporary continental table d'hôte menu, which is changed daily, alongside an exquisite à la carte menu.

The restaurant, with stunning views over the Ponsbourne estate, has three individual rooms which combine to form an exclusive yet versatile room. Enjoy a quite corner, sit in front of the marble fireplace or relax by the grand piano.

Ponsboune Park Hotel is also an ideal venue for weddings, private and business functions with a range of rooms to suit all requirements.

REDEMPTION
SIGNATURE

10% discount
Any day, lunch or dinner

See terms & conditions on page 7. Expiry date: 31 December 2004

George & Dragon

Watton-at-Stone (Map Ref: **162** F4) (English/British) (Average Price: £18.00)

High Street, Watton-at-Stone
Hertford SG14 3TA
Tel: 01920 830285
Fax: 01920 830042
pub@georgeanddragon-watton.co.uk
www.georgeanddragon-watton.co.uk

*Winners of the 'Good Pub
Guide - Hertfordshire
Dining Pub of the Year'
category no less than five
times*

Opening hours

M-Th 11.00-3.00 6.00-11.00
Fri   11.00-3.00 5.30-11.00
Sat   11.00am -   11.00
Sun   12.00noon - 10.30

Food served

M-F 12.00-2.00 7.00-10.00
Sat 12.00-2.00 7.00-10.00
Sun 12.00-2.00 no food
Booking is advisable at
weekends.

Food style
English/British

Features & facilities
Disabled facilities
Garden/Outside eating area
Non-smoking area
Real ales
Special diets catered for
Vegetarian dishes
Wines - extensive selection
Child friendly
- Children's menu
- High chairs

The George and Dragon has held an excellent reputation for the quality of its food for more than 40 years. In July 2001 when it changed hands after 28 years the head chef, Jessica Tatlow, and her husband Peter took over. Jessica had been head chef for over six years during which time the pub won the 'Good Pub Guide - Hertfordshire Dining Pub of the Year' category no less than five times and has been recommended in several national newspapers.

The building itself is full of charm offering a gently sophisticated atmosphere, with exposed beams, attractive old tables and chairs in the bar areas, an interesting mix of modern and old prints, large bay windows and real fires. The public bar has an oak panelled dado and old photographs of the pub and village. Real ales are well kept and there is always a guest ale on offer.

A good range of food is available in the bar areas and dining rooms, offering everything from a light snack to a full dining experience. The food is beautifully presented and the service is friendly and professional. In addition to the varied menu, an extensive wine list offers a choice of over 40 wines to suit all tastes. The main dining area seats around 30 people and the small dining room offers a cosy environment for those who want a more intimate experience.

Outside is a Petanque pitch, patio area with heaters and a pretty shrub screened garden.

The Five Horseshoes

1 Church Road
Little Berkhamsted
Hertford SG13 8LY
Tel: 01707 875055
Fax: 01707 876250

With over 50 dishes there
is something for every
palate and pocket

Opening hours

M-F 11.00am - 11.00pm
Sat 11.00am - 11.00pm
Sun 12.00noon - 10.30pm

Food served

M-F 11.00am - 10.00pm
Sat 11.00am - 10.00pm
Sun 12.00noon - 9.30pm

Food style

English/British, specialising
in fish and seafood

Features & facilities

Disabled facilities
Garden/Outside eating area
Non-smoking area
Real ales
Vegetarian dishes
Wheelchair access
Wines - extensive selection

Directions

From Hertford: take the
B158 (Lower Hatfield Road),
after 4.5 miles turn left up
Robins Nest Hill. After 1
mile turn left again at the
War Memorial into Church
Road and the pub is on your
left just after the church.

Landlord and landlady Tommy Takacs and Dee
Gallagher have run the Five Horseshoes for the
past 18 months. You are always guaranteed a
warm and friendly welcome from Tommy, Dee
and their staff.

Situated in the lovely village of Little
Berkhamsted the pub overlooks the cricket
ground and boasts picturesque gardens complete
with water feature.

Step inside and step back in time. The open log
fires, low beams and traditional hops hanging
from the ceilings all add to the homely
atmosphere. Candles are a big feature with one
on every table and large church candles on the
walls give an atmospheric glow to the bar and
dining areas.

The wide ranging menu, with over 50 dishes
displayed on blackboards around the walls,
consists of traditional English dishes such as
sausages, bubble 'n' squeak or fish and chips
through to fillet steak au poivre. An extensive
selection of fresh fish is delivered daily from the
coast. There is also a lighter snack menu for
those with a smaller appetite.

The vast menu is complemented by an extensive
wine list with all wines sold by the glass or
bottle plus a choice of real ales.

This is one of the most popular eateries in the
area and well worth a visit.

Hitchin

including Kimpton, Preston, Redcoats Green

Hitchin Highlights

- The Priory

- Hitchin Museum

- The Sun Hotel

- The Hitchin British Schools Educational Museum

For further information about this town and the surrounding villages contact:

Hitchin Initiative
27 Church Yard
Hitchin SG5 1HP
Tel: 01462 453335
Email: htci@hitchin.net

Opening hours:
Mon-Sat 9.30am - 1.30pm
Closed Sundays and Bank Holidays

*Information kindly supplied by
the Hitchin Initiative*

Bustling and lively with a great sense of community, Hitchin is alive to its traditions as a historic market town but is also a modern, thriving town and local forum.

It's a great town for dining with more than forty town centre coffee shops, restaurants and pubs, bars and hotels offering cuisine for all tastes from the exotic to the reassuringly traditional. As well as the town's two theatres – The Market Theatre in Sun Street and the Queen Mother Theatre in Walsworth Road – there is a host of live music venues that regularly stage all kinds of sounds from folk, rock and jazz to big band and classical.

History, such as the St Mary's Church, which dates back to 792AD and is the largest parish church in the county, co-exists happily alongside these modern day attractions. The town's museums range from local interest to international renown, for example The British Schools Educational Museum.

Next to the church the home counties' largest market is held every Tuesday and Saturday for general goods such as fruit and vegetables and fashion clothing and on every Friday stalls sell a cornucopia of antiques and bric-a-brac.

Hitchin is a mere 35 minutes by rail from London Kings Cross and much less from Cambridge, just a 15 minute drive from Luton Airport via the A505 and an hour's drive from London on the A1(M) or M1.

Restaurant Mirage

(Mediterranean) (Average Price: £25.00)

Hitchin (Map Ref: **162** E3)

56 Bancroft
Hitchin SG5 1LL
Tel: 01462 615019
Fax: 01462 615019
www.restaurantmirage.com

A truly Mediterranean experience

Opening hours

M-F 12.00-2.00 6.30-11.00
Sat 6.30-11.00
Sun Closed

Food style
Mediterranean

Features & facilities
Disabled facilities
Vegetarian dishes
Weddings/Private functions
Wheelchair access
Wines - extensive selection

Restaurant Mirage opened in October 2002 and offers a truly Mediterranean experience which can normally only be found abroad.

Attilio and Numan have each brought a wealth of experience to the restaurant which is combined to bring you the finest in Mediterranean cuisine through the extensive menu. With influences from France, Italy, Spain and Turkey, there is something for everyone, all set in a warm and friendly atmosphere.

Suitable for both business and pleasure, Attilio and Numan will ensure that your dining experience will be met with the uniqueness that the Mediterranean is now so famous for.

In addition to offering first class food and the very finest wines, Restaurant Mirage also offers unique first class entertainment every Thursday evening and on selected Saturday evenings. Ricardo Curbelo, Latin American harpist, invites you to sit back and enjoy a very special dining atmosphere, to make your evening even more special.

Parking is easy and the local train station is only a 10 minute walk away.

The restaurant does get very busy so book early to avoid disappointment.

The White Horse

Kimpton (Map Ref: 162 E4)

22 High Street
Kimpton, Hitchin SG4 8RJ
Tel: 01438 832307
Fax: 01438 833842
thewhitehorsepub@aol.com
www.whitehorsekimpton.co.uk

Extensive menu including fresh fish and vegetarian choices

Opening hours

M-F	12.00-2.30	6.00-11.00
Sat	12.00-2.30	6.00-11.00
Sun	12.00-4.00	7.00-10.30

Food served

M	No food served
T-F	12.00-2.00	7.00-9.00
Sat	12.00-2.00	7.00-9.00
Sun	12.00-2.00

Food style
English/British

Features & facilities
Garden/Outside eating area
Log Fire
Non-smoking area
Real ales
Wines - extensive selection

Peter and Janet Johnson and their staff always extend a very warm welcome to visitors to this delightful country pub.

The Grade II listed building dates back to the 16th century and has its own priest hole secured behind the bar.

You will find it set in the picturesque village of Kimpton – a few miles from Harpenden, Codicote and Hitchin.

Enjoy a relaxed meal in the restaurant area which has a cosy log fire on winter evenings. In the summer months, dine on the pretty sun deck or just sit back and enjoy a pint or two of the award winning ales - Peter is the McMullen Master Cellarman for 2003. There is an extensive menu which includes fresh fish dishes, vegetarian choices and superb quality meat dishes. Fresh local produce is used whenever possible.

The pub runs occasional theme nights and also has the usual range of pub games and activities with a fun quiz night every Tuesday.

REDEMPTION
SIGNATURE

10% Discount
Tues-Fri Lunch & Tues-Thur Dinner

See terms & conditions on page 7. Expiry date: 31 December 2004

Redcoats Farmhouse Hotel & Restaurant

(Modern British)   (Average Price: £35.00)   **Redcoats Green** (Map Ref: **162** E3)

Redcoats Green
Little Wymondley
Nr Hitchin, SG4 7JR
Tel: 01438 729500
Fax: 01438 723322
sales@redcoats.co.uk
www.redcoats.co.uk

The atmosphere is one of warmth, comfort, luxury and tranquility

Opening hours

Breakfast	7am - 9am
Lunch	12pm - 2pm
Dinner	7pm - 9pm

Food style
Modern British,
International, à la carte and
table d'hôte.

Features & facilities
Child friendly
 - High chairs
 - Children's menu
Disabled facilities
Garden/Outside eating area
Licensed for civil marrages
Non-smoking area
Special diets catered for
Vegetarian dishes
Weddings/Private functions
Wheelchair access
Wines - extensive selection

The farmhouse dates back to 1450 and since the turn of the century it has been owned by the same family. Set in 4 acres of beautiful gardens and with unspoiled views over the countryside, it is difficult to believe that this stunning country retreat is only 5 minutes from the A1(M) and 20 minutes from the M1 and M25.

The atmosphere of Redcoats Farmhouse is one of warmth, comfort, luxury and tranquility. The exposed beams, open fireplaces and traditional farmhouse decor add to its ambience and all the staff are very attentive and welcoming.

You have a choice of restaurants for either lunch, dinner or supper in the conservatory. The head chef and his team only ever produce the very best in traditional homemade cuisine and all the produce is sourced to achieve the maximum level of quality and freshness. A sample menu can be viewed on the restaurant's website.

If you are looking for a venue to hold your wedding, somewhere to hold a conference or business meeting or if you simply want to relax and unwind, then this is the place for you.

REDEMPTION
SIGNATURE

10% Discount (FOOD ONLY)
Monday to Thursday, lunchtime and evening

See terms & conditions on page 7. Expiry date: 31 December 2004

McAllisters Cafe Ecosse

Hitchin (Map Ref: **162** E3) (Modern British) (Average Price: £20.00)

12 Bridge Street
Hitchin SG5 2DE
Tel: 01462 431661

*You're sure to have an
enjoyable time,
everytime!*

Opening hours

M-F 6.30pm - 11.00pm
Sat 6.30pm - 11.00pm
Sun 1.00pm - 7.30pm

Food style
Modern British

Features & facilities
Garden/Outside eating area
Vegetarian dishes
Weddings/Private functions
Wines - extensive selection

Cafe Ecosse has been a popular restaurant since it opened in December 1999. In Feburary 2002 it became part of the McAllister Holdings group which also includes The White Lion at Walkern and The Plough in Radwinter, Saffron Walden.

The restaurant is located in a 17th Century building, which retains many of its original features, for example, exposed beams and the original hearthplace which is large enough for customers to have dinner in! Towards the rear of the property is a lovely conservatory, which seats up to 50, and has relaxing views of the beautiful 'Italian style' courtyard garden.

The extensive modern British menu changes regularly and ranges from pot au haggis or antipasto of cured Highland beasts to Arbroath smokie or prime Angus steaks. Combine this with well chosen wines, a choice of 14 malt whiskies, an unusual range of bottled beers and the fantastic service, and you're sure to have an enjoyable time, everytime!

The Red Lion

The Green
Preston, Hitchin SG4 7UD
Tel: 01462 459585

*It was Britain's first
'community owned' pub
in 1983*

Opening hours

M-F 12.00-2.30 5.30-11.00
Sat 12.00-3.00 5.30-11.00
Sun 12.00-3.00 7.00-10.30

Food served

M-F 12.00-2.00 7.00-9.00
       excluding Tuesdays
Sat 12.00-2.00 7.00-9.00
Sun 12.00-2.00

Food style
English/British with an
emphasis on homemade

Features & facilities
Garden/Outside eating area
Real ales
Vegetarian dishes
Wines - extensive selection

This is a delightful county pub run by Tim and Jane Hunter. A freehouse, it is Britain's first 'community owned' pub and is therefore very popular with the local residents.

You will always find a warm and friendly atmosphere whatever the weather or time of year. There is a large and well maintained garden for you to enjoy in the summer and cosy log fires to relax by in the winter months.

The traditional homemade food is available for lunch and dinner except on Tuesday and Sunday evening. On Sunday there is always a traditional roast but with vegetarian options available.

The menu includes homemade pies, game dishes when in season, fresh fish and a good range of other dishes including vegetarian options plus a good selection of puddings. Light snacks of fresh sandwiches and ploughmans are always available.

The Red Lion serves an ever changing range of real ales and it won the North Herts CAMRA Pub of the Year in 2000 and 2001 and the Herts CAMRA Pub of the Year in 2000.

The village of Preston is south of Hitchin and is signposted from the B651.

Bridge Street Bistro

Hitchin (Map Ref: 162 E3)   (English/British)   (Average Price: £16.00)

26 Bridge Street
Hitchin SG5 2DF
Tel: 01462 440072

*This small bistro oozes
charm and character*

Opening hours

M-F   12.00 - 2.30 6.30 - 12-00
Sat   7.00 - 12-00
Sun   12.00 - 2.30

Food style
English/British

Features & facilities
Non-smoking area
Weddings/private functions
Wheelchair access
Wines - extensive selection

For the past four years the Bridge Street Bistro has been run by Albert, who is not only the proprietor but also the chef.

Previously, he was the head chef at the famous Victorian music hall, 'The Players Theatre Club' in London's West End where he cooked regularly for many of the celebrities who frequented the Club.

Found in a back street away from the main High Street, this small bistro oozes charm and character. From the moment you walk through the door you are made to feel welcome. The service is superb and the food, as you would expect, impeccably presented.

The restaurant is spacious with a warm and inviting decor. The modern open plan design ensures that wherever you're seated you will see Albert and his team at work.

Bridge St.
Bistro

This is a venue that can cater for every occasion be it a cosy meal for two, or a business meeting through to a large birthday gathering you won't be disappointed.

Hoddesdon

Why the name Hoddesdon? No-one seems to know for sure but since its listing in the Domesday Book as Hodesdone the name has remained.

Like so many others in the county, Hoddesdon is a market town and every Wednesday has been market day since the cattle market began in 1886, although the town is believed to have held regular markets since 1253 when Henry III granted the charter for a market on Thursdays and a three-day annual fair on St Martin's Day.

The prosperity generated by the market combined with the coaching trade on the London-Cambridge road meant that by the 18th century the town was an important coaching centre with more than thirty inns and hostelries, some of which still stand, such as The Golden Lion, the White Swan and the Salisbury Arms.

One of the inns was a handy base for the activities of a certain 'broad shouldered, pockmarked man' who used to hold up travellers at gunpoint and steal their riches on the road from Hoddesdon to Ware in the 1730s. His name, as you might have guessed, is Dick Turpin.

The centrepiece of the market to this day is the clock tower, which stands on the site of the 14th century Chapel of St Katherine, whose 16th century bell is still housed in the clock tower.

Finally, a little known Hoddesdon curiosity merits a passing mention. Despite its long history, the town did not become a parish in its own right until 1844, before which it straddled the border between Great Amwell and Broxbourne. Even today, outside the local Co-Op department store there is a strangely split paving stone which marks the former parish boundary.

The Huntsman

Hoddesdon (Map Ref: **166** G5)   (**English/British**)   (**Average Price: £15.00**)

Goose Green
Hoddesdon EN11 8SN
Tel: 01992 443294
Fax: 01992 470821
www.thehuntsmangoosegreen.co.uk

*A traditional
Hertfordshire country
pub*

Opening hours

M-f 12.00-2.30 5.00-11.00
Sat 12.00noon - 11.00pm
Sun 12.00noon - 10.30pm

Food served

M-Tu 12.00-2.00
W-Fr 12.00-2.00 7.00-9.00
Sat 12.00-2.00 7.00-9.00
Sun 12.00-2.30

Food style

English/British

Features & facilities

Child friendly
- High chairs
- Children's menu
Garden/Outside eating area
Real ales
Vegetarian dishes

The Huntsman is a genuine family-run Hertfordshire country pub. It has been offering refreshments since before 1750. Known as The Green Man until 1980, the pub is a well kept secret, tucked away in the tiny hamlet of Goose Green on a quiet backroad just a mile west of Hoddesdon (via Lord Street) and 3 miles from Hertford (via Mangrove Road). In 1980 the pub was used to record a hilarious Two Ronnies TV sketch – why not ask to see it when you visit? The traditional food is well cooked with generous portions.

Inside you will find a real log fire, genuine oak beams, darts, pool, shove ha'penny at one end of the pub and a secluded area set aside for dining at the other.

A selection of cask conditioned ales, bottled beers, bottled and draught lagers are always available. The range of wines on offer are limited but reasonably priced. It has a large safe garden, together with something of a menagerie – currently two pot bellied pigs, three goats, three Shetland ponies, chickens, and doves. And, of course, the resident ghost (really) but keep that to yourself!

Kings Langley

including the village of Chipperfield

Kings Langley Highlights

- The Tomb of Edmund de Langley

- The Grand Union Canal

This historic village has an illustrious royal past. It acquired its name in Norman times when Eleanor of Castille, the wife of Edward I, bought the Langelei or long meadow, that lined the banks of the River Gade, to create a royal hunting park and built a royal palace at the top of nearby Langley Hill. Edward II added a Dominican Friary and later, Edward III used the palace as the base for the Government of England during the Black Death in 1349.

Sadly, most of the palace was destroyed by fire in 1431 but Kings Langley's royal legacy lives on, even if the Kings themselves do not, in the tomb of Edmund de Langley, the first Duke of York and brother of the Black Prince, which rests in the village's 15th century church.

It's not all history though. Today, the village has a thriving high street with many varied shops, a library, community centre as well as primary and secondary schools. On the sports front, the village has an active bowls club and its cricket and football clubs have recently completed new modern facilities. The village also has many community groups and societies and every June stages the annual carnival on the common. For many years until his death, Kings Langley was the home of renowned jazz musician and radio presenter Benny Green.

In close proximity to the M25, Kings Langley also has good rail links with London. The Grand Union canal, which reached the village in 1797, forms the border with Abbots Langley to the East.

Information kindly supplied by Dacorum Information Centre

La Casetta

Kings Langley (Map Ref: 165 D6) (Italian) (Average Price: £22.00)

18 High Street
Kings Langley WD4 8BH
Tel: 01923 263823
spencer@lacasetta.co.uk
www.lacasetta.co.uk

"The essence of what a restaurant is supposed to be"

Opening hours

Mon Closed
Tu-F 12.00noon - 11.00pm
Sat 7.00pm - 11.00pm
Sun First Sunday of the month Gourmet Lunch from 12.30pm

Food style
Italian but with other modern European influences

Features & facilities
Non-smoking area
Special diets catered for
Vegetarian dishes
Wines - extensive selection

La Casetta is set in a 16th century cottage in the heart of Kings Langley, 2 minutes from the M25, junction 20. The menu offers flavours from the Mediterranean with strong Italian influences and it changes with the seasons every 6-8 weeks.

It has been awarded Restaurant of the Year 2002 and its Chef, Marco Major, was awarded Chef of the Year 2002. More recently, it won Small Business of the Year 2003 in the Watford and North West London Business Awards, for the way its menu, wine list and quality of service have developed.

The Daily Telegraph's Jan Moir describes La Casetta as, "The essence of what a restaurant is supposed to be, deserving of its awards and its increasing popularity. A place that serves good quality ingredients correctly cooked and served in generous portions at a very fair price".

La Casetta means 'The Little House' and as long as it continues to offer excellent quality and value, it will remain one of the region's favourite places to enjoy a friendly meal.

Food quality, presentation and service are all excellent and it is well worth a visit.

The Boot Inn

Chipperfield (Map Ref: **164** C6)

Tower Hill, Chipperfield,
Kings Langley WD4 9LN
Tel: 01442 833155

This is a great pub for all the family with a paddock, small playground and often a bouncy castle

Opening hours

M-F	12noon - 11.00pm
Sat	12noon - 11.00pm
Sun	12noon - 11.00pm

Food served

M-F	12.00-2.30	6.30-9.30
Sat	12.00-2.30	6.30-9.30
Sun	12.00-2.30	6.30-9.30

Food style
English/British

Features & facilities

Child friendly
- High chairs
- Children's menu
Garden/Outside eating area
Non-smoking area
Private functions
Real ales
Special diets catered for
Vegetarian dishes
Wheelchair access
Wines - extensive selection

Nigel Durrant is celebrating his first year as the owner of this traditional country pub. The building dates back to 1610 and was originally two cottages. It still retains much of its old charm, enhanced by a wonderful display of hanging baskets in the summer.

Behind the pub is a paddock-style garden, with an unusual combination of three rescue ponies, two old buses used for fun parties and a small marquee with its own outside bar. Inside, the traditional exposed beams are decorated with a range of bric-a-brac including a collection of old caps and helmets.

The Boot Inn offers a varied menu with dishes such as pan fried calves liver, grilled sea bass, cajun red snapper and a variety of steaks complemented by a reasonable wine list and guest ales.

This is a great pub for all the family, with a small adventure playground and often children's entertainment and a bouncy castle - well worth a drive through the beautiful countryside in this part of Hertfordshire.

REDEMPTION
SIGNATURE

Free bottle of house wine
tables of 4 or more Monday-Thursday

See terms & conditions on page 7. Expiry date: 31 December 2004

Letchworth

Letchworth Highlights

- The black squirrels of Norton Common

- Broadway and the Town Square

- The Spirella Building

- Museum and Art Gallery

For further information about this town and the surrounding villages contact:

Letchworth Garden City
Tourist information Centre
33-35 Station Road
Letchworth Garden City SG6 3BB
Tel: 01462 487868
Fax: 01462 485532

Opening hours:
Mon-Sat 9.30am - 4.30pm
excluding bank holidays

Information kindly provided by the Letchworth Garden City Tourist information Centre

The world's first garden city was inspired by a book called 'Tomorrow A Peaceful Path to Real Reform' by Ebenezer Howard, a visionary who believed he had the solution to urban overpopulation, rural depopulation and the resultant poor housing conditions. His concept, of carefully planned 'garden cities', aimed to combine the health benefits associated with living in the countryside with all the comforts and amenities of urban life.

In 1903 Howard's vision became a reality and the great social experiment that was Letchworth Garden City began in earnest.

Unfortunately, though, it was impossible to toast the city's launch in the traditional way because Howard believed that liquor was inappropriate in a garden city. When it was put to the vote, the new residents agreed and in 1907 Letchworth saw what was probably another first: an alcohol-free pub! The Skittles Inn (now the Settlement Education Centre) was opened to provide the atmosphere of a pub but without the temptation.

You can still see the meticulous planning that went into the town in the magnificent approach to the centre along the tree-lined Broadway and, as you'd expect from a carefully planned town, Letchworth has plenty to offer in recreational facilities, including the central Howard Park with its children's pool, a modern leisure centre, open-air swimming pool and cinema. Last, but not least, is Norton Common, home to Letchworth's famous rare black squirrels which were first sighted in 1944 and have featured on national television many times since.

Just 37 miles from London, Letchworth is within easy driving distance of all the London airports via the M25 and M1, and London's King's Cross station is just 32 minutes away by rail.

Sagar Tandoori Restaurant

(Indian) (Average Price: £21.00)

Letchworth (Map Ref: **162** E2)

48 Broadway
Letchworth
Tel: 01462 675771

*A popular restaurant
recommended by The
Good Curry Guide*

Opening hours
M-F 5.30pm - 11.00pm
Sat 12.00-2.00 5.30-11.30
Sun 12.00noon - 11.00pm

Food style
Indian

Features & facilities
Child friendly
 - Children's menu
 - High chairs
Disabled facilities
Non-smoking area
Private functions
Special diets catered for
Vegetarian dishes
Wheelchair access
Wines - good selection

The Sagar Tandoori Restaurant has been under the same ownership and management since 1994. It is also recommended by The Good Curry Guide and has a good local reputation with many regular customers.

The Mughal cuisine is based on traditional recipes from the north of India. One of the most popular dishes is Khanshama Jhol – marinated chicken fillets, cooked in a sauce with freshly prepared herbs and spices and green chillies.

The modern design of the restaurant is light and airy with comfortable, well spaced seating. There is a small, cosy bar area where you can enjoy a drink before your meal. The staff are friendly and efficient. There is also a separate room available for small parties and private functions.

The restaurant boasts a selection of over 90 different liqueurs including some wonderful calvados and armagnacs.

REDEMPTION
SIGNATURE

Free bottle of house wine
for table of 4, Monday-Thursday

See terms & conditions on page 7. Expiry date: 31 December 2004

Shapla White

Letchworth (Map Ref: **162** E2)　　　　　(Indian)　(Average Price: £8.50)

71 Station Road
Letchworth
Tel: 01462 682820

*Gourmet night on a
Wednesday is very
popular*

Opening hours

M-F 12.00-2.30　5.30-12.00
Sat 12.00-2.30　5.30-12.00
Sun 11.00-10.00

Food style

Indian

Features & facilities

Child friendly
Private functions
Vegetarian dishes
Wheelchair access
Wines - extensive selection

Shapla White has been under the current ownership and management for just over a year.

It is a popular restaurant, conveniently situated near Letchworth station. The table settings are stylish with crisp linen table cloths, folded napkins and old fashioned style oil lamps.

The food is based on a range of traditional Nepali and Indian recipes. The Nepali dishes are quite spicy and capture the true aroma and taste of this Great Himalayan region. Popular choices include the padina chicken, a medium strength dish grilled and cooked slowly in a special sauce and the tandoori king prawn chapila cooked in a clay oven with a hot and spicy sauce.

The gourmet night on a Wednesday evening is always very popular and with a five course meal for £9.95 it is excellent value for money.

The restaurant is popular so it is advisable to book for the Wednesday gourmet nights and at weekends. The Shapla White also offers a takeaway service with free deliveries on all orders over £10 to the local area.

REDEMPTION
SIGNATURE

15% Discount

any time, any day, except Gourmet meals.

See terms & conditions on page 7. Expiry date: 31 December 2004

Much Hadham
and Little Hadham

including Perry Green

Sitting prettily in the valley of the River Ash, Much Hadham is arguably the best looking village in Hertfordshire with its elegant, predominantly Tudor and Georgian houses. In fact the late Sir Nikolaus Pevsner described the straggling linear settlement as, 'visually probably the most successful village in the county....' and goes on to say that, '...the main street is a delight from beginning to end.'

Much Hadham probably owes its name to a far more ancient moniker – that of Hadda, the Saxon victor in the battle against the Danes that took place in nearby Widford. The earliest records date from 946AD when a childless Saxon queen left her Hadham land to the Bishops of London, one of whom was happy to escape the plague-ridden capital and build himself a summer palace in the village.

For such a small place there is a lot to see, including The Lordship, a mansion at the north end of the High Street with its stable block featuring a clock cupola and wealth of half-timbered and pargetted 17th and 18th century cottages, and St Andrew's church featuring the greeting 'This is the gate to heaven' over the door.

You may also notice two unusual carved 'head stops' of a king and queen on the church's tower doorway. These are by the late sculptor Henry Moore, who once lived in Much Hadham and whose works can be viewed by appointment at the Henry Moore Foundation in nearby Perry Green.

The Bull Inn & Carters Restaurant

Much Hadham (Map Ref: 163 H4) (English/British) (Average Price: £15.00)

High Street
Much Hadham SG10 6BU
Tel: 01279 842668

A traditional country pub, transformed into a light and airy restaurant which retains many of its original features

Opening hours

Tu-F 12.00-3.00 6.00-11.00
Sat 12.00-3.00 6.00-11.00
Sun 12.30-4.00 7.00-10.30

Food served

Tu-F 12.00-2.00 6.30-9.15
Sat 12.00-2.00 6.30-9.15
Sun 12.30-3.00

Food style

English/British

Features & facilities

Child friendly
 - Baby changing facilities
 - High chairs
 - Children's menu
Disabled facilities
Garden/Outside eating area
Non-smoking area
Private functions
Real ales
Special diets catered for
Vegetarian dishes
Wheelchair access

There was a change of ownership and management in December 2002 which saw the start of a complete refurbishment for The Bull. The new manager, Simon Lawrence, and his team have transformed this traditional country pub into a light and airy restaurant and bar. It still retains many of its original features with exposed beams, wooden floors and open fires but these blend superbly with the fresh, new decor.

The Summerhouse Bar in the large rear garden is now open. The garden is excellent for children as it includes a play area and a miniature petting area with rabbits, chipmonks, lovebirds and Hector the miniature Shetland pony.

The new menu contains many favourites such as hot chicken with bacon and avocado salad or local pork and leek sausages with mash and onion gravy. The Bull also offers a good selection of vegetarian dishes.

There is ample car parking and the pub is close to the award winning Hopley's Nursery; another excuse for a very pleasant afternoon in this lovely part of Hertfordshire.

The Hoops Inn

Perry Green
Much Hadham SG10 6EF
Tel: 01279 843568
Fax: 01279 843637
the.hoopsinn@btconnect.com
www.thehoopsinn.co.uk

*A varied menu of home
cooked food*

Opening hours

M-F	12.00-2.30	6.30-11.00
Sat	12.00-3.00	6.00-11.00
Sun	12.00noon - 10.30pm	

Food served

M-F	12.00-2.00	6.30-9.30
Sat	12.00-2.30	7.00-10.00
Sun	12.15 -	8.00

Food style
English/British

Features & facilities
Child friendly
 - High chairs
Garden/outside eating area
Non-smoking area
Special diets catered for
Vegetarian dishes
Weddings/private functions

The Hoops Inn dates back to the 17th century and is a delightful, traditional English country pub set in the rural village of Perry Green near the Henry Moore Foundation. You can reach Perry Green from Bishop's Stortford, Ware or Harlow - see the pub's website for directions.

This friendly, family run hostelry includes a large garden with a tranquil pond and a small, secure paddock. Horse riders are welcome to leave their horses in the paddock whilst they themselves graze in the bar or restaurant.

The home-cooked menu is varied, drawing inspiration from home and abroad. Popular dishes include steak sizzlers served on a cast iron sizzle platter, prawn stir fry sizzler with mushrooms, onions, peppers and spices or the special Hoops tagliatelle - chicken fillet and smoked bacon in a cream and mushroom sauce with ginger and coriander, served with tagliatelle. The Hoops Inn also offers a range of bar snacks.

From the bar, you can choose from a range of cask conditioned beers, lagers and wines.

This is a popular area for walkers who are welcome to park and assemble in the car park in the morning, pre-order lunch, set off for a walk and then return to pre-reserved tables for lunch.

The Nags Head

Little Hadham (Map Ref: 163 H4)   (Fish/Seafood)   (Average Price: £12.00)

The Ford
Little Hadham
Tel: 01279 771555

Fish and seafood are a speciality and the menu boasts an extensive choice of over 27 fish dishes

Opening hours

M-F	11.00-3.00	6.00-11.00
Sat	11.00-3.00	6.00-11.00
Sun	12.00-3.30	7.00-10.30

Food served

M-Th	12.00-2.00	6.00-9.00
Fri	12.00-2.00	6.00-9.30
Sat	12.00-2.00	6.00-9.30
Sun	12.00-2.00	7.00-9.00

Food style
Fish/Seafood with a range of traditional British fayre

Features & facilities
Child friendly
 - High chairs
 - Children's menu
Garden/Outside eating area
Non-smoking area
Real ales
Vegetarian dishes

This Grade II listed building has been a public house or coaching inn since 1595 and part of the building dates back even further to the 1400s.

With exposed beams and traditional features, the building oozes the charm and history of a traditional English country pub.

For the past 21 years it has been run by the Robinson family and you can be certain of a warm welcome.

Fish and seafood are a speciality and the menu boasts an amazingly extensive choice of over 27 fish dishes. If you're not a fish lover, the extensive à la carte menu offers over 30 dishes from which to choose.

Whilst you're choosing from the large selection of meals available, why not sample one or two of their worldwide selection of wines - you'll be spoilt for choice.

From Thursday to Sunday booking is highly recommended and definitely worth it.

Potters Bar

including Cuffley

Potters Bar Highlights

- The De Havilland Heritage Museum of Aviation

- Wrotham Park Manor House

Potters Bar is a recent arrival on the map of Hertfordshire. In historical terms, there is not much to be said, since most of the town's growth has come about in fairly recent years.

The 1930s saw rapid expansion with much house building and the establishment of a second shopping centre by the railway station at Darkes Lane. This was followed after World War Two with the development of large housing estates to accommodate the overspill of residents from north London areas such as Edmonton and Tottenham.

Even as recently as the 1920s, the now bustling Darkes Lane was just a quiet country lane but the High Street was part of the Great North Road, which accounts for the presence of ancient 17th century coaching inns such as The Green Man and The Robin Hood.

Well-connected to London, with the M25 on its doorstep, Potters Bar is a busy, modern town with all the modern amenities you'd expect and an excellent selection of pubs and restaurants.

There is also a host of places well worth visiting in the surrounding areas such as the De Havilland Heritage Museum of Aviation and the Roman ruins of Verulamium at nearby St Albans.

Pubali Tandoori

Potters Bar (Map Ref: **165** F6)   (Indian) (Average Price: £15.00)

90 High Street
Potters Bar
Tel: 01707 655272

*Award winning
restaurant serving a
wonderful array of
Tandoori dishes*

Opening hours

M-F	12.00-2.30	6.00-11.30
Sat	12.00-2.30	6.00-11.30
Sun	12.00-2.30	6.00-11.30

Food style
Indian

Features & facilities
Non-smoking area
Special diets catered for
Vegetarian dishes
Wheelchair access
Wines - extensive selection

Three times winners of the Hertsmere Curry Chef of the Year competition, Dilwar Hussain and his team maintain the highest standards of cuisine year-on-year.

Conveniently located in Potters Bar High Street, this unpretentious restaurant serves some of the best Tandoori and Indian dishes in the county.

The restaurant has recently been refurbished and offers a relaxed and comfortable environment. All the staff are very friendly and welcoming.

All the food is freshly prepared and cooked on the premises using the finest ingredients and spices. The popular house specialities include chicken jeera marinated in black pepper and mustard seed, king prawn jhalfryzi, lamb chana and a unique vegetable thali.

Dilwar has managed this restaurant since 1980 and maintains the same enthusiasm and commitment to customer service and quality food as he did over twenty years ago.

Well worth a visit.

REDEMPTION
SIGNATURE

Free bottle of house wine
for tables of 4 or more, Mon-Thurs.

See terms & conditions on page 7. Expiry date: 31 December 2004

(Chinese) (Average Price: £15.00)

16 Station Road,
Cuffley, Potters Bar EN6 4HT
Tel: 01707 875341
       01707 876801

A range of expertly prepared Peking and Cantonese dishes.

Opening hours

Mon 6.00pm - 11.30pm
Tu-Fr 12.00-2.30 6.00-11.30
Sat 12.00-2.30 6.00-11.30
Sun 12.00noon - 11.30pm

Food style

Chinese, specialising in Peking and Cantonese cuisine

Features & facilities

Child friendly
 - High chairs
Non-smoking area
Private functions
Vegetarian dishes
Wines - good selection

This is a very popular restaurant with a strong local following.

The cuisine is based on a range of Peking and Cantonese dishes and it is always expertly prepared and well presented. Popular dishes include the special mixed satay, roast duck with Chinese mushrooms and bamboo shoots and the fresh baked crab cooked in a selection of sauces.

The restaurant is smart and spacious with stylish decor and comfortable seating. There is a small bar area where you can enjoy a drink before your meal. The staff are friendly and efficient.

Sundays are now very busy when diners can enjoy a buffet for just £9.00 for a starter, main course and dessert. There is always a range of at least 20 of the most popular dishes to choose from.

The wine selection and traditional chinese beers are reasonably priced.

Table 88

Potters Bar (Map Ref: 165 F6)

(Chinese) (Average Price: £15.00)

88 High Street
Potters Bar EN6 5AT
Tel: 01707 647888

*Predominantly Peking
and Szechuan style with
some additional dishes
from Malaysia*

Opening hours

M-F	12.00-2.30	6.00-11.00
Sat	12.00-2.30	6.00-11.00
Sun	12.00-2.30	6.00-11.00

Food style
Chinese

Features & facilities
Child friendly
Private functions
Vegetarian dishes
Wheelchair access
Wines - extensive selection

Wing Lai is celebrating his first year as owner of this new restaurant.

The interior is bright and modern with wooden floors, whitewashed walls and stylish, contemporary seating. The atmosphere is relaxed and the staff are professional and attentive.

The food is predominantly Peking and Szechuan in style with some additional dishes from Malaysia. Favourite dishes include soft shelled crabs in salt and pepper; lobster and ginger spring onions and Malaysian kam heung chilli chicken. Vegetarians are also well catered for with a good selection of dishes from which to choose.

Table 88 offers a range of wines with some notable bottles from Italy imported by a specialist wine merchant.

Upstairs, via a spiral staircase, a private function room caters for parties of up to 26 people.

REDEMPTION
SIGNATURE

10% Discount (Sun-Thurs)
excludes special menu and set lunch menu

See terms & conditions on page 7. Expiry date: 31 December 2004

Radlett

Radlett Highlights

- The Radlett Centre

- Christ Church (an early Sir George Gilbert Scott design)

Although there has been a settlement on this site since Roman times and its High Street is part of the famous Watling Street Roman Road, there is little trace of the village of Radlett in the records until the 18th century.

In fact, much more modern events were responsible for Radlett's rapid growth since the First World War – namely its excellent road and rail links.

These days it is an attractive, quiet 'dormitory' settlement, something of an 'urban village' with a good range of shops, pubs and restaurants alongside some attractive flint and brick 'Gothick' cottages dating from 1852 on the station approach.

Hinting at a future more wakeful than that of the average 'dormitory' town is a new and welcome addition to Radlett's amenities, the Radlett Centre. This joint venture between Aldenham Parish Council, Hertsmere Borough Council and Hertfordshire County Council accommodates the parish council offices as well as providing a superior village library, a community hall with theatre and concert facilities, meeting rooms and a bar and refreshment area.

Abalone Seafood Restaurant

Radlett (Map Ref: 165 E6)   (Fish/Seafood)   (Average Price: £25.00)

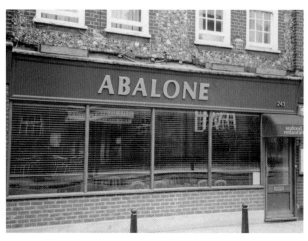

243 Watling Street
Radlett WD7 7AL
Tel: 01923 855994
Fax: 01923 855994
www.abalone-restaurant.co.uk

*Some of the best seafood
in Hertfordshire*

Opening hours

Mon Closed
Tu-F 6.15pm - 10.00pm
Sat 6.15pm - 10.00pm
Sun 6.15pm - 10.00pm

Food style

Specialising in fish and seafood but with a range of other Mediterranean dishes

Features & facilities

Vegetarian dishes
Wines - good selection

Owner and chef Peter Shek has been creating superb, well presented dishes for over 20 years. He loves cooking and discussing food with people who enjoy 'real food', so when the kitchen closes for the evening and guests are enjoying the end of their meal, Peter frequently appears from the kitchen to discuss the menu with his customers.

Abalone specialises in serving an extensive range of quality fresh fish and other seafood delights - the lobster bisque is wonderful. There is a menu but your best bet is to check the blackboard for special dishes which use the best seasonal fish available from the market that day. Abalone also caters for other tastes with a variety of chicken, duck, beef and vegetarian dishes.

Peter draws his inspiration from around the world and the style ranges from modern British, through to Mediterranean and even includes some Japanese.

A varied selection of fine wines to complement your meal at reasonable prices are available.

Abalone is conveniently located on Radlett High Street (Watling Street), just 2 minutes' walk from the train station. Free parking is available nearby. Radlett is less than 10 minutes' drive from M1 junction 5 and about the same from M25 junction 22.

The Dining Rooms

(English/British) (Average Price: £20.00)

Radlett (Map Ref: **165** E6)

78 Watling Street
Radlett WD7 7NP
Tel: 01923 855341

*Wine and dine whilst you
enjoy an art exhibition*

Opening hours
M-F 9.00-3.00 5.30-late
Sat 9.00am - late
Sun 9.00am - late

Food served
All day menu available
every day, à la carte menu
at the following times:
M-F 12.00-3.00 5.30-10.00
Sat 12.00noon - 10.00pm
Sun 12.00noon - 10.00pm
Breakfast available from
9.00am to 11.45am

Food style
English/British

Features & facilities
Air conditioned
Child friendly
 - High chairs
Live jazz on Sun/Thursdays
Live Blues on Wednesdays
Non-smoking area
Vegetarian dishes
Wines - extensive selection

The recently refurbished Dining Rooms offers a
unique concept for dining in Hertfordshire: an
opportunity to enjoy a high quality art exhibition
with an equally high quality dining experience.

The art is displayed around the walls of the
restaurant and a recent exhibitor included Rolf
Harris. Limited edition prints and paintings are
available for sale, either unmounted or framed.

The main dining area is smartly furnished with a
large round table as a central feature.

Food is available throughout the day although
you're more than welcome to sit and enjoy one
of the flavoured coffees, cappucino or a fruit
milkshake whilst you view the exhibition.

The main à la carte menu offers a wide choice of
traditional English cuisine using fresh local
ingredients. One of the most popular parts of the
menu is the large steak board which uses the
finest Scottish beef. The Sunday roast is
available throughout the day.

This is a restaurant that caters for everyone and
all occasions, be it a quick snack, coffee with
friends or the full dining experience, and it has
the added benefit of some beautiful art for you
to enjoy as well. The art exhibition changes each
month so look out for your favourite artists.

Rickmansworth

including Chandlers Cross, Croxley Green and Sarratt

Back in Saxon times, Rickmansworth was a lone farmstead sandwiched between the ridge of the Chiltern Hills and a marshy mere in the flood plain of the rivers Colne, Chess and Gade.

It was this wetland environment that led to Rickmansworth's rise when London found itself short of water and plans were agreed to make up the shortfall from Rickmansworth's three rivers. This entailed turning the River Colne into what became known in 1778 as the Grand Junction Canal, connecting London and the Midlands. This later fed into the Grand Union Canal, which reached Rickmansworth in 1786, and the modern town began to grow and grow, nourished by a plentiful waterborne trade.

Some of the new businesses that sprang up made direct use of the newly constructed waterway, such as Salter's Brewery, whilst others fed on the influx of trade from the waterways and opened shops on the High Street.

Today, the High Street is packed with shops, pubs and restaurants, including many famous high street names. The town is still growing, thanks largely to the speedy half-hour rail link to London, and the town now boasts a number of tourist attractions, including the Watermeet Theatre, Moor Park sports and recreational centre, the medieval St Mary's church and, of course, the Grand Union Canal, now used mainly by leisure craft.

The Plough

Belsize
Sarratt WD3 4NP
Tel: 01923 262261
realfood@theploughbelsize.com
www.theploughbelsize.com

*If you like real ales, real
food - and real people -
you'll love The Plough!*

Opening hours

Mon 6.00pm - 11.00pm
Tu-Fr 12.00noon - 3.00pm
             6.00pm - 11.00pm
Sat 12.00noon - 11.00pm
Sun 12.00noon - 10.30pm

Food served

Mon Closed lunch 7.30-9.30
Tues 12.00-2.00   7.30-9.30
W-Sat 12.00-2.00   6.30-8.30
Sun 12.00-3.00

Food style

Traditional British but with
Indian cuisine on Monday
and Tuesday evenings.

Features & facilities

Child friendly
 - Children's menu
Garden/Outside eating area
Non-smoking area
Private functions
Vegetarian dishes
Wines - extensive selection

Situated in the hamlet of Belsize, between Sarratt
and Chipperfield, on the edge of the Chess Valley,
The Plough offers a selection of real ales, quality
wines and home-cooked meals in the friendly
atmosphere of a traditional, village pub.

With ample car parking, a beer garden and separate
dining area, it caters for everyone from hikers and
bikers, to drinkers and diners. And, during the colder
months, the real log fires make The Plough even
more welcoming!

With the emphasis on quality and freshness, the
extensive week-day lunch menu often features
home-baked favourites such as steak 'n' ale pie,
shepherd's pie and lasagne. On Sundays, as well as
two roasts, vegetarian and fish options are also
offered, followed by a choice of home-made
desserts and English cheeses. From Wednesday to
Saturday evening, the dinner menu combines supper
dishes of beer-battered cod, bangers and mash, chilli
and curries, with seasonal meat, fish and game
platters - cooked to order and served with freshly
prepared vegetables or salads.

On Monday and Tuesday evenings, Sarratt residents
Ahmed and Veena Jamal, prepare and serve
authentic, home-cooked dishes from the Lucknow
region of northern India - real curries!

Clarendon Arms

Chandlers Cross (Map Ref: 165 D7)   (English/British)   (Average Price: £14.00)

Redhall Lane
Chandlers Cross
Rickmansworth WD3 4LU
Tel: 01923 262924
Fax: 01923 261480
www.theclarendon.co.uk

A reputation for good pub food at a reasonable price

Opening hours

M-F	11.00am - 11.00pm
Sat	11.00am - 11.00pm
Sun	12.00noon - 10.30pm

Food served

Mon	12.00noon - 5.30pm
Tu-Fr	12.00noon - 8.30pm
Sat	12.00noon - 8.30pm
Sun	12.00noon - 5.30pm

Food style
English/British

Features & facilities
Garden/Outside eating area
Non-smoking area
Real ales
Vegetarian dishes
Wines - extensive selection

This delightful country pub has been under new management since August 2002. Since then, it has developed a reputation for providing good quality, home cooked, traditional English 'pub grub' at a reasonable price. The food is complemented by a selection of real ales, lagers and wines.

Its rural location makes it very popular with walkers, attracted by the various footpaths through the local woods.

The Clarendon Arms holds a barbeque on every Bank Holiday - a great day out for all the family with a selection of meats and salads in true South African or Antipodean fashion - weather cannot be guaranteed though!

Lunch time and evenings are busy, especially at the weekends. It is advisable to book but bookings are not taken on a Sunday for the traditional Sunday roast, nor for outside tables.

A range of bar snacks - baguettes, jacket potatoes and sandwiches - are also served.

REDEMPTION
SIGNATURE

10% Discount
Monday lunch, Tues-Sat lunch or dinner

See terms & conditions on page 7. Expiry date: 31 December 2004

Curry Garden

141 Uxbridge Road
Rickmansworth WD3 7DW
Tel: 01923 776900/770622
Fax: 01923 773563
www.currygardenricky.co.uk

A wonderful new menu which covers the culinary traditions of various regions of the Indian sub-continent

Opening hours

M-F	12.00-2.30	5.30-11.30
Sat	12.00-2.30	5.30-11.30
Sun	Buffet 12.00-5.00	

Food style

Indian

Features & facilities

Non-smoking area
Vegetarian dishes

Established in 1979, the Curry Garden has always had a reputation for quality food with excellent service. Now, with a newly refurbished modern interior and an extensive new menu, it is set to go from strength to strength.

The bar with its striking uplighting effect, indoor water feature, tables with crisp linen and coloured oil filled lamps creates a welcoming atmosphere. Using all their experience the owners have redesigned the menu which now covers the culinary traditions of various regions of the Indian sub-continent.

There are new balti and vegetarian dishes with unique flavours and tastes and recipes, which come from some of the top hotels in India.

The staff are friendly and helpful and happy to explain any dish on the menu.

The Sunday Buffet for £6.95 is excellent value – you can eat as much as you like from a generous selection of favourite dishes.

Coach & Horses

Croxley Green (Map Ref: **165** D7)　　(English/British)　(Average Price: £14.00)

The Green, Croxley Green
Rickmansworth
Tel: 01923 774457
Fax: 01923 774757

*The log fire is a warm
and welcoming sight in
the winter*

Opening hours

M-F　11.00am-11.00pm
Sat　11.00am-11.00pm
Sun　12.00noon - 10.30pm

Food served

M-F　12.00-2.30　6.00-9.30
Sat　12.00-3.00　6.00-9.30
Sun　12.00-3.30

Food style
English/British

Features & facilities
Child friendly
- High chairs
- Children's menu
Disabled facilities
Garden/Outside eating area
Non-smoking area
Private functions
Real ales
Special diets catered for
Vegetarian dishes
Wheelchair access

This attractive Grade II listed pub overlooks 'The Green' in Croxley Green. The pub dates back to the early 1700s with all the character and charm you would expect.

Enjoy the summer sunshine in the garden at the back of the pub and in the winter the real log fire is a welcoming sight and provides a cosy and relaxed atmosphere.

Lunch or dinner is available every day of the week, except on Sunday evenings, and you can choose from a set menu or the specials board which changes regularly.

It's advisable to book for Sunday lunch when a selection of roasts plus a range of special dishes are always available.

For something different, why not try a game of Petanque, which is similar to French Boules – the staff will explain the rules!

REDEMPTION
SIGNATURE

10% discount
any evening

See terms & conditions on page 7. Expiry date: 31 December 2004

Royston

including Melbourn and Reed

Royston is a small market town with a history that goes back two millennia to the Roman construction of Ermine Street. Royston grew up at the Street's intersection with Icknield Way, another Roman Road, which was marked by a wayside cross at the base of which was the Royse Stone: a two tonne rock left behind by the receding glaciers of the Ice Age, which still has pride of place in 'Royse Stone' town centre.

Among many other historical monuments too numerous to mention, perhaps the most fascinating is the Royston cave, which draws visitors from all over the world. The walls of this bell-shaped man-made chamber hollowed out of the chalk beneath Melbourn Street are decorated with esoteric medieval carvings, attributed to the Knights Templar, whose secret conclave it is thought to have been, and so dated at around 1300 AD.

But there is much more to Royston than its past. These days, it's a vibrant market town packed with pubs, restaurants, shops and sports facilities nestling in some of the county's most beautiful countryside. As a regular entrant in the Anglia-in-Bloom competition, the town's often found festooned with flowers, hanging baskets and features the award-winning Priory Memorial Gardens, which are renowned as the 'jewel in the crown' of the town.

Despite its rural atmosphere, Royston's easy accessible with the A1(M) and M11 close by and frequent rail services from London King's Cross and Cambridge stations.

*Information kindly supplied by
Royston Town Council*

The Cabinet

Reed (Map Ref: 163 G2) | Trans-Atlantic | | Average Price: £28.00 |

High Street
Reed, Nr Royston SG8 8AH
Tel: 01763 848366
Fax: 01763 849407
thecabinet@btopenworld.com
www.thecabinetinn.co.uk

*This is one restaurant you
cannot afford to miss*

Opening hours
Mon Closed
Tu-Fr 12.00-3.00 6.00-11.00
Sat 12.00-3.00 6.00-11.00
Sun 12.00noon - 6.00pm

Food style
A compilation of the best
of French, English and
Trans-Atlantic cuisine

Features & facilities
Child friendly
- High chairs
Disabled facilities
Garden/Outside eating area
Non-smoking area
Private functions
Real ales
Special diets catered for
Vegetarian dishes
Wines - extensive selection

From the outside this could be any ordinary, pretty
village pub. Inside however, TV chef, Paul Bloxham,
and his team have worked their magic.

The building is over 500 years old and still has
many original features, such as exposed beams, an
open fireplace and tiled flooring, all superbly
enhanced by the recent refurbishment. The
comfortable high-backed leather dining chairs in
the bar area and the elegant dining room with its
sparkling glasswear, crisp linen, low lighting and
freshly cut flowers add to the ambience.

The menu, as you would expect, is delicious. Sample
dishes include pan fried seabass with fennel sauce
and tempura baby fennel, and to follow rump of
salt marsh lamb, poached garlic flan and rosemary-
pepper broth, accompanied by one of the many fine
wines on offer, and to finish walnut dusted coffee
mousse with honeycomb.

Outside is a new al fresco dining area with open
plan kitchen, wood burning rotisserie and patio
heaters.

All in all, whether it is lunch or dinner for two, a
bespoke wedding reception or business meeting,
this is one restaurant you cannot afford to miss.

the **Cabinet**

Sheene Mill

Station Road, Melbourn
Nr Royston SG8 6DX
Tel: 01763 261393
Fax: 01763 261376
info@sheenemill.co.uk
www.sheenemill.co.uk

This restaurant and hotel are of the finest calibre

Opening hours

M-F	12.00-2.30	7.00-10.30
Sat	12.00-2.30	7.00-10.30
Sun	12.00-3.00	Eve. closed

Food style
English/British

Features & facilities
Child friendly
 - High chairs
Conservatory
Garden/Outside eating area
Non-smoking area
Special diets catered for
Vegetarian dishes
Weddings/Private functions
Wheelchair access
Wines - extensive selection

Sheene Mill is owned by celebrity chef and award winner Steven Saunders and his wife, Sally.

As you would expect from someone who has won awards from Young Chef of the Year at the age of 25, through to the accolade of Master Chef of Great Britain, this restaurant and hotel are of the finest calibre.

The modern, brasserie style restaurant is set in beautiful surroundings with an idyllic millpond serving as a backdrop for diners. It offers exquisite cuisine and a friendly, professional service.

All the menus reflect Steven's strong conviction that the use of organic, local, fresh seasonal produce and British ingredients are essential and once you have tasted the results we think you will agree.

If your time is limited, the Conservatory is ideal. It offers tempting light snacks, coffee and exceptional wines and is open all day. Or, if you wish to celebrate in style, a visit to the Champagne Bar is a must, offering cocktails, organic draught beers and naturally, champagne!

Sheene Mill caters for everything from business conferences, to individual bespoke wedding receptions, through to special occasions or a romantic meal for two.

St Albans

including London Colney and Redbourn

St Albans Highlights

- Verulamium Museum

- Cathedral and Abbey Church of
  St Albans

- The de Havilland Aircraft
  Heritage Museum of Aviation

- The Clock Tower

- Gardens of the Rose

**For more information on the
town and surrounding villages
contact:**

St Albans Tourist Information
Centre
Town Hall, Market Place
St Albans
Tel: 01727 864511
Fax: 01727 863533
Email: tic@stalbans.gov.uk

Summer opening hours:
Mon-Sat 9.30am - 5.30pm
Sun   10.00am - 4.00pm

Winter opening hours:
Mon-Sat 10.00am - 4.00pm
Sun   Closed

Bank Holidays 10.00am-4.00pm

*Information kindly provided by
the St Albans Tourist information
Centre*

The city is named after Saint Alban, the first Christian martyr, whose shrine is within the Abbey. People have been making pilgrimages to St Albans for centuries and, as you approach its historic heart, overlooked by the impressive cathedral and abbey church, it's easy to see why.

The sense of drama started in around 140AD in the original Roman city of Verulamium and the Roman Theatre – the only example of its kind in Britain – where Roman citizens once watched dancing, wrestling, armed combat and gladiatorial contests. Nearby are the remains of a row of shops, a villa complete with hypocaust heating system and a sacred shrine, which all date from the first century AD.

St Albans is a city where tradition rubs along effortlessly with the hip and the happening – yet nothing seems out of place. The thousand year-old street market clusters around the city's host of ancient churches, pubs and coaching inns – many of them haunted – alongside high fashion and specialist shops, street cafés and restaurants featuring almost every style of cuisine you could name. The list of entertainments events at the three theatres is endless and the city stages numerous festivals and historic re-enactments throughout the year. In short, after two thousand years, St Albans is still the place where history meets today!

The city is so compact that it's easy to tour on foot and although it might seem a million miles from the crowds and crush of London, St Albans is just minutes from the M1 and M25 and a mere twenty minutes from London by rail.

Magnolia Restaurant, Sopwell House

(English/British)   (Average Price: £25.00)   **St Albans** (Map Ref: 165 E6)

Sopwell House
Hotel, Country Club & Spa
Cottonmill Lane, Sopwell
St Albans AL1 2HR
Tel: 01727 864477
Fax: 01727 844741
enquiries@sopwellhouse.co.uk
www.sopwellhouse.co.uk

*This fine dining
restaurant is renowned
for acclaimed cuisine*

Opening hours

M   Closed
Tu-F   12.00-3.00   7.00-10.00
Sat   7.00-10.00
Sun   12.00-2.30   7.00-9.30

Food style
English/British

Features & facilities
128 bedrooms
Berjerano's Brasserie
Child friendly
 - High chairs
Conferences & banquetting
Disabled facilities
Health & beauty club
Non-smoking area
Special diets catered for
Vegetarian dishes
Private functions
Wedding & Civil Marriage
 Licence
Wheelchair access
Wines - extensive selection

The Magnolia Restaurant is built around the boughs of 100 year old Magnolia trees, set within the 4 star hotel. Awarded 2 AA Rosettes, this fine dining restaurant is renowned for acclaimed cuisine plus discreet and knowledgeable service, in elegant surroundings.

Executive Chef Ian Penn combines flavour, freshness and imagination, whilst also providing value for money.

A typical table d'hôte menu, which changes on a weekly basis, could include dishes such as Mediterranean vegetable terrine with an olive oil and balsamic dressing; pan fried skate wing, black butter, creamed potatoes and leek fondue with a dessert of raspberry and white chocolate cheesecake with a raspberry coulis.

There is also an extensive à la carte selection and a traditional Sunday lunch. Fresh, local produce is used in all menus, with a choice of fish and vegetarian options. Special dietary requirements can be met, by prior arrangement.

A special Christmas menu is available throughout December and the restaurant is open for New Year's Eve and other seasonal celebrations.

Please note the management respectfully ask that dress is smart/casual and that the restaurant is a non-smoking environment. The hotel offers a comfortable lounge and extensive gardens where smoking is permitted.

The Jade Garden

St Albans (Map Ref: **165** E6) (Chinese) (Average Price: £16.50)

16-24 Spencer Street
St Albans AL3 5EG
Tel: 01727 856077
www.thejadegarden.co.uk

*A wide selection of
Cantonese dishes for you
to choose from*

Opening hours

M-F 12.00noon - 2.15pm
     5.30pm - 11.30pm
Sat 12.00noon - 11.30pm
Sun 1.00pm - 11.30pm

Food style

Chinese - specialising in
Cantonese dishes

Features & facilities

Non-smoking area
Private parties
Vegetarian dishes
Wines - extensive selection

The Jade Garden was opened by owner Kim Lau when he emigrated from Hong Kong in 1969. As such, it is the oldest Chinese restaurant in the city remaining under the same ownership.

One of the most popular eateries in St Albans, it is situated in one of the city's listed buildings, just off the main market place.

The atmosphere in the restaurant is enhanced by the tasteful decor and efficient, friendly service.

It is fully licensed and offers a range of old and new world wines at a reasonable price.

Cantonese cuisine has developed in popularity over the past few years and the comprehensive à la carte menu has been developed to incorporate a wide range of dishes for you to enjoy. The table d'hôte menu changes regularly so you will always find something new to try.

The table d'hôte menu is available for groups of up to 12 people but individually tailored menus for parties of up to 40 people can be arranged.

The Jade Garden offers an excellent choice, but Kim also reserves a part of his menu for some of the simple, traditional dishes which he first served when he opened in 1969 and which are still popular with diners today.

The Waffle House

St Albans (Map Ref: **165** E6)

(Belgian Waffles) (Average Price: £12.00)

Kingsbury Watermill
St Michael's Street
St Albans AL3 4SJ
Tel: 01727 853502
Fax: 01727 730459

The fresh waffles come out of the irons crisp and hot

Opening hours

M-F 10.00am - 6.00pm
Sat 10.00am - 6.00pm
Sun 11.00am - 6.00pm
Closed at 5.00pm in the winter

Food style

Contemporary continental, specialising in Belgian Waffles

Features & facilities

Child friendly
- High chairs
Disabled facilities
Garden/Outside eating area
Non-smoking area
Vegetarian dishes
Watermill museum
Gift shop

The Waffle House has been under the same ownership for over 20 years and is located in beautiful surroundings, right on the river Ver.

It is famous for its waffles which are always crisp and hot straight out of the irons and freshly made to order using home-made batter, with the best quality organic free-range eggs and organic stone ground flour. A variety of sweet and savoury toppings are available, the most popular include free-range ham with cheese and mushroom, or fresh seasonal fruit with cream. Don't forget to check out the daily specials board.

The Waffle House is unlicenced but try a real milkshake, Lavazza espresso coffee or choose from the selection of teas and you won't be disappointed.

It is always busy and runs on a strictly 'first come first served' basis with no bookings taken.

The 16th century building has many original features and also houses the working Watermill Museum and gift shop. See the watermill at work with the wheel and cogs turning as well as a range of early tools and implements.

REDEMPTION
SIGNATURE

10% Discount
off bills of £5 per head or more, Mon-Fri

See terms & conditions on page 7. Expiry date: 31 December 2004

109

Wagamama

St Albans (Map Ref: 165 E6)

(Pan Asian) (Average Price: £11.00)

St Christophers Place
St Albans
Tel: 01727 865122
Fax: 01727 867264
www.wagamama.com

The menu is a delightful mix of pan-Asian dishes and there really is something for everyone

Opening hours
M-F 12.00noon - 11.00pm
Sat 12.00noon - 11.00pm
Sun 12.30pm - 10.00pm

Food style
Pan Asian

Features & facilities
Child friendly
- High chairs
Disabled facilities
Non-smoking area
Special diets catered for
Vegetarian dishes
Wheelchair access

From professionals to students, media types to celebrities, everybody continues to enjoy the Wagamama experience.

Wagamama is based on the traditional ramen bars of Japan and, although the menu is a delightful mix of pan-Asian dishes, there really is something for everyone here - steaming bowls of ramen (noodles in soup) with meat, seafood or vegetarian choices, plenty of rich dishes, the spicy and the not so spicy.

There is a wide selection of side dishes, which you shouldn't confuse with starters. When each dish is ordered at Wagamama it is tapped into an electronic handheld PC and sent straight to the kitchen by radio signals, so your food is being cooked as soon as the words are out of your mouth. Now that's fresh ...

The restaurant is clean, minimalist and non-smoking. Seating is at canteen-style tables and the service is friendly, attentive and fast.

An 'eat out' option is available.

wagamama

Giovanni's

St Albans (Map Ref: **165** E6)

The Black Lion
198 Fishpool Street
St Albans AL3 4SB
Tel: 01727 859250

Opened in 1993,
Giovanni's provides the
best-known Italian dishes
prepared with the finest
ingredients

Opening hours

Mon	6.30pm - late	
Tu-F	10.30-2.30	6.30-late
Sat	10.30-2.30	6.30-late
Sun	Closed	

Food served

Mon	6.30pm - 10.30	
Tu-F	12.30-2.30	6.30-10.30
Sat	12.30-2.30	6.30-10.30
Sun	Closed	

Food style
Italian

Features & facilities

Child friendly
Private functions
Real ales
Special diets catered for
Vegetarian dishes
Wines - good selection

Giovanni's is set within The Black Lion Pub, in Fishpool Street, which claims to be England's oldest pub site - an ale house dating back to 60AD. The attractive pub is within strolling distance of many of the city's famous attractions and there is plenty of parking.

Giovanni's is most certainly authentic and a must for a connoisseur of Italian cuisine and as it states on the menu *"Though the roots of Italian cuisine stem from the Romans, the gastronomy of Giovanni's Restaurant remains unique unto itself"*.

All the dishes are prepared to order using only the freshest and finest ingredients. The deep love of cooking and food is complemented by the relaxed ambience of the management and staff.

When it comes to wine, Giovanni's can tempt the enthusiast with a glorious indulgence of full bodied, robust, intense and concentrated wines.

Cafe des Amis

St Albans (Map Ref: **165** E6)   (Fish/Seafood)   (Average Price: £25.00)

31 Market Place
St Albans AL3 5DL
Tel: 01727 853569
margaret@cafedesamis.fsnet.co.uk

One of the widest choices
of fresh fish and seafood
in Hertfordshire

Opening hours

M-F   10.00-3.00   7.00-late
Sat   9.30-5.00   7.00-late
Sun   Closed

Food style

Modern European
specialising in fish and
seafood

Features & facilities

Disabled facilities
Non-smoking area
Private functions
Special diets catered for
Vegetarian dishes
Wheelchair access
Wines - extensive selection

Margaret Hayward has owned and run this popular establishment since 1996. This is probably the smallest restaurant in this guide, tucked away behind a half shop façade in St Albans Market Place.

The style is one of a relaxed continental bistro where you can enjoy anything from a coffee to a full à la carte meal.

The food style is modern European but Cafe des Amis specialises in fish and seafood. Everything is fresh using only the finest produce available from the market each day. Just a selection of the most popular dishes include the fresh mussels marniére or provençal, deep fried whitebait finished with finely diced onions and paprika, whole dover sole or skate wing with white wine and capers or black butter.

Cafe des Amis also serves a range of steak dishes using the finest Scottish beef. If you like steak, share a Chateaubriand cooked with a mushroom and red wine sauce - delicious!

You have to be careful not to walk right past this restaurant and it does look like a small cafe but the à la carte menu, served from 7.00pm every day except on Sundays, is wonderful and deserves its good local reputation.

Gastrodome

14-16 Heritage Close
St Albans AL3 4LB
Tel: 01727 851941
aw@gastrodome.com
www.gastrodome.com

*Good quality, healthy
and nutritious food at a
reasonable price*

Opening hours

M-F 12.00noon - 10.30pm
Sat 12.00noon - 10.30pm
Sun 12.00noon - 8.00pm

Food style
International

Features & facilities
Child friendly
- High chairs
- Children's menu
Disabled facilities
Garden/Outside eating area
Non-smoking area
Private functions
Special diets catered for
Vegetarian dishes
Wheelchair access
Wines - extensive selection

Gastrodome offers an eating experience that successfully combines prompt service with healthy, high quality and freshly cooked food, all at the best possible value.

It specialises in chicken dishes but also offers excellent mature steaks, fantastic lamb, fresh fish, superb sausages, noodles and salads.

Very child friendly, there is a promotion for children of 12 years of age and under who, if they bring an adult with them for lunch or dinner on any day, can choose a free meal from the kids menu. Only one free child meal per adult meal purchased.

Gastrodome's loyalty and nutrition programme offers lots of benefits for members which include food and beverage discounts, complimentary bottles of champagne, nutritional advice and menu guidance tailored to the member's needs.

Food has never tasted so good. The restaurant only uses the best cereal fed chicken, the fish is steamed or grilled and the meat chargrilled to minimise the need to use extra oils during cooking.

There is a substantial wine list of fine wines at affordable prices from well selected wine producers who are still passionate about wines.

Free starter or dessert
when you order a main course

REDEMPTION
SIGNATURE

See terms & conditions on page 7. Expiry date: 31 December 2004

113

Claude's Creperie

St Albans (Map Ref: 165 E6) (French) (Average Price: £17.50)

15 Holywell Hill
St Albans AL1 1EZ
Tel: 01727 846424

*A family-run restaurant
located in a Grade II
listed building which
offers unpretentious
home-cooked food*

Opening hours

Mon Closed
Tu-Th Closed 6.00-10.30
Fri 12.00-3.00 6.00-11.00
Sat 10.30am-11.00pm
Sun 10.30am-10.00pm

Food served

Last orders one hour before
closing

Food style

French

Features & facilities

Child friendly
 - High chairs
Outside courtyard
 eating area
Real ales
Special diets catered for
Vegetarian dishes
Wines - extensive selection

This family-run restaurant is located in a Grade II
listed building and offers unpretentious home-
cooked food, a relaxed friendly atmosphere and
romantic candle-lit evenings.

It specialises in sweet and savoury pancakes. The
savoury crêpes and galettes can be filled with
special ingredients inspired by international
cuisine or you can choose your own filling from a
huge list of ingredients which caters for all tastes.

Alternatively, you can have an omelette with any
filling or one of a range of main course salads and
Haagen Dazs ice cream to follow.

Claude's Creperie offers an extensive range of
reasonably priced French wines or there is the
option to 'bring your own' with corkage charged
at £3 per bottle. There is also a large range of
French ciders and unusual bottle-fermented beers.

At the weekend there is a brunch menu with
breakfast, moules with French bread, scrambled
eggs, filled croissants and baguettes.

CLAUDE'S

Chequers Inn

1 St Albans Road
Redbourn, St Albans AL3 7AD
Tel: 01582 792359

*An ideal place whether
you're after a quick bite
or a full meal*

Opening hours

M-F 11.00am - 11.00pm
Sat 11.00am - 11.00pm
Sun 12.00noon - 10.30pm

Food served

M-F 11.00am - 10.00pm
Sat 11.00am - 10.00pm
Sun 12.00noon - 9.30pm

Food style

English/British

Features & facilities

Disabled facilities
Garden/Outside eating area
Non-smoking area
Real ales
Special diets catered for
Vegetarian dishes
Wheelchair access
Wines - extensive selection

The Chequers has been run by husband and wife team Steve and Nicky Woodhead for the past 3 years. It exudes the character of a traditional British pub. Originally a 14th century coaching station, the earliest known reference to The Chequers is on a map dated 1760, when it formed part of the Fish Street Farm owned by Lord Verulam.

The pub offers an extensive array of freshly cooked food with choices displayed on blackboards around the bar and restaurant. Fresh fish is the house speciality but whatever you choose it is prepared and served with the same enthusiasm amd commitment.

The pub is open all day, every day and food is served throughout the day, so it is an ideal place to eat whether you're after a quick bite or a full meal. The staff are always friendly and you are never rushed, creating a relaxed and homely atmosphere.

There's the choice of hand-pulled fines ales including regular guest ales such as Woodford Great Eastern or Cains Formidable and an extensive wine list with 20 wines offered by the glass.

With such an extensive menu there is something for everyone here and it is excellent value for money.

Colney Fox

London Colney (Map Ref: 165 E6)   (English/British)   (Average Price: £15.00)

Barnet Road
London Colney
St Albans AL2 1BL
Tel: 01727 820902

*Good British food served
all day, every day*

Opening hours

M-F	11.00am - 11.00pm
Sat	11.00am - 11.00pm
Sun	12.00n00n - 10.30pm

Food served

M-F	12.00noon - 10.00pm
Sat	12.00noon - 10.00pm
Sun	12.00noon - 9.30pm

Food style

English/British

Features & facilities

Child friendly
- High chairs
- Children's menu
Disabled facilities
Garden/Outside eating area
Non-smoking area
Real ales
Vegetarian dishes
Wheelchair access
Wines - extensive selection

Conveniently situated on the outskirts of St Albans and close to junction 22 of the M25 this is a popular pub, smartly decorated inside and with a large garden.

The building dates back to the 17th century and was formerly a coaching inn. It is said to be haunted but the warm welcome you receive from manager Jason Nash and his team is anything but spooky.

The food is good quality traditional British fayre and the menu changes four times a year to incorporate the freshest produce from each season. Current favourites include crab and salmon fishcakes; beef, mushroom and ale pie or a classic chicken caesar salad. There is also a good selection of vegetarian dishes.

Wines are reasonably priced and there is a varied selection to choose from.

The pub also has accommodation with 13 bedrooms all with ensuite facilities.

REDEMPTION
SIGNATURE

Free bottle of house wine
for table of 4 or more, Mon-Fri

See terms & conditions on page 7. Expiry date: 31 December 2004

Stevenage and Knebworth

including Ardeley, Codicote and Datchworth

Stevenage was the first of the 'new towns', thanks to the New Towns Act of 1946 and has one of Europe's first traffic-free precincts. It is a new place with an ancient name: one where the new has been built over and around the old and yet where there is a surprising wealth of history to be unearthed. For example, Six Hills Way, one of the town's major arteries is named after the six tumuli or burial chambers built two millennia ago by the Romans and left untouched until the Saxons settled and built the settlement of Sithenaece, which means 'strong oak'.

The town's history is full of celebrated names – such as Samuel Pepys, who stayed in The Grange, which bears a commemorative plaque, and EM Forster, who grew up in Stevenage and based parts of Howard's End on the town, renaming it 'Hilton'.

Less illustrious, but more amusing, is the fact that Stevenage was used as a location for the film Boston Kickout, in which one character boasts, 'I've been kicked out of every club in Stevenage!' to which another replies, 'but there are only two'.

The new town is packed with entertainment and leisure facilities from clubs (there are more than two now!), pubs and bowling to countless restaurants, the Gordon Craig Theatre and associated leisure centre, the Leisure Park with its multi-screen cinema, the swimming pool and a lot more besides. Nearby Stevenage Old Town rolls along at a slower pace and still has all its ancient village charm as well as a wealth of pubs and restaurants that are full of character.

The Jolly Waggoner

Ardeley (Map Ref: **162** F3)　　　　Average Price: £25.00

Ardeley, Nr Walkern
Stevenage SG2 7AH
Tel: 01438 861350

*A 500 year old pub with
exposed beams and
quarry tiled floor*

Opening hours
Tu-F　12.00-2.30　6.30-11.00
Sat　12.00-3.00　6.30-11.00
Sun　12.00-3.00　7.00-10.30

Food served
Tu-F　12.00-2.00　6.30-9.30
Sat　12.00-2.00　6.30-9.30
Sun　12.00-2.00

Food style
English/British

Features & facilities
Child friendly (over 7 yrs)
Garden/outside eating area
Non-smoking area
Real ales
Special diets catered for
Vegetarian dishes
Wines - extensive selection

The Jolly Waggoner and its Rose Cottage Restaurant has been run by Darren Perkins and chef Scott Halliwell for over 12 years.

The attractive pink painted building sits in the middle of the pretty, traditional English village of Ardeley. Over 500 years old, the interior is rich with exposed beams, quarry tiled floors and antique fixtures and fittings and is further enhanced in the winter months by the open log fire.

You can dine in the bar area of the Jolly Waggoner where you can enjoy the delights of fresh crab; mussels; omelette Arnold Bennett; calves liver with a Roquefort and horseradish sauce; fantastic salads or simply a superb sandwich.

The traditional bar also offers a full range of draught beers and real ales.

Alternatively, you can dine in the quaintly named Rose Cottage Restaurant. Enjoy such delights as Arbroath smokies, fillet of lamb en-croute or roasted fillet of seabass.

The Jolly Waggoner also has well maintained gardens at the front and back of the pub.

The Bell Motel & The Vines Cafe

(Modern European) (Average Price: £15.00) Codicote (Map Ref: **162** E4)

65 High Street
Codicote, Stevenage SG4 8XD
Tel: 01438 821600
Fax: 01438 821700
info@thebellmotel.co.uk
www.thebellmotel.co.uk

*High standards of good
traditional English and
modern European cuisine*

Opening hours

M-F 12.00-2.30 7.00-9.30
Sat 12.00-2.30 7.00-9.30
Sun 12.00-2.30

Food style
Modern European

Features & facilities
Child friendly
 - Children's menu
 - High chairs
Disabled facilities
Garden/Outside eating area
Non-smoking area
Private functions
Special diets catered for
Vegetarian dishes
Wheelchair access
Wines - extensive selection

If business or pleasure takes you to Stevenage, Hatfield, Welwyn Garden City or Hitchin, The Bell Inn Motel, situated in the beautiful rural village of Codicote and just 5 minutes from the A1, is an ideal place to stop.

The Vines Cafe restaurant has recently been refurbished with stylish wooden tables and comfortable chairs, tasteful decor and ceiling fans.

The restaurant offers high standards of good traditional English and modern European cuisine from the à la carte menu or see the blackboard for the specials of the day.

Popular dishes include smoked chicken with avocado on a bed of salad leaves drizzled with a lime and coriander dressing; peeled prawns stir fried with peppers, tomatoes, onions, cucumber and wild rice lightly spiced with soy sauce, Tabasco and ginger or the chargrilled Caribbean-style chicken with a pepper, pineapple and coconut sauce. There is also a traditional bar menu.

There is a very good selection of vegetarian dishes with four starters and six main courses to choose from. The mushroom, red pepper and stilton bake cooked in a creamy sauce topped with sliced potatoes and grated cheese is very popular.

The motel is privately owned and has 25 tastefully decorated bedrooms with en suite facilities.

Coltsfoot Country Retreat

Datchworth (Map Ref: **162** F4)　　(English/British)　(Average Price: £27.50)

Coltsfoot Lane, Bulls Green
Datchworth, Knebworth SG3 6SB
Tel: 01438 212800
Fax: 01438 212840
info@coltsfoot.com
www.coltsfoot.com

*A charming and relaxing
country-style retreat*

Opening hours
M-F　7.00pm - 11.30pm
Sat　7.00pm - 12.00am
Sun　closed

Food served
M-F　7.00pm - 9.45pm
Sat　7.00pm - 9.45pm
Sun　closed

Food style
English/British

Features & facilities
Disabled facilities
Garden/outside eating area
Non-smoking area
Special diets catered for
Vegetarian dishes
Weddings/private functions
Wheelchair access
Wines - extensive selection

Coltsfoot stands proudly in 40 acres of Hertfordshire countryside. Once a working farm dating back to the 16th century, it has been skillfully renovated into a country style retreat. It retains all its old charm with a stylish courtyard and a converted barn which dates back to 1836.

Set in a rural atmosphere, the courtyard, buildings and interior design create a warm and relaxing atmosphere for business or pleasure. In winter, the ambience is completed with a brightly burning log stove.

The restaurant offers a fine selection of quality food and wines, enjoyed in a comfortable and spacious environment overlooking the courtyard or open countryside. The extensive à la carte menu is mostly derived from fresh local produce. Service is always of a high standard.

There is a comfortable lounge and bar area for drinks before your meal and coffee afterwards.

The hotel offers 15 luxury individual suites - each designed in a different style - and all with en suite bathrooms with either claw foot tubs, ultra modern suites or hydrotherapy air bath. All rooms have a CD player and Virgin Vie toiletries.

There is an 18-hole golf course nearby and the hotel is happy to book a round for you.

Aroma

Stevenage (Map Ref: **162** F3)

Stevenage Leisure Park
Kings Way
Stevenage SG1 2UA
Tel: 01438 352183
Fax: 01438 354007
Email: mail@thearoma.co.uk
www.thearoma.co.uk

An excellent value 'eat as much as you like for a fixed price' restaurant

Opening hours

M-F 12.00-3.00 6.00-11.30
Sat 12.00-3.00 5.30-11.30
Sun 12.00-4.00 5.00-10.30

Food style
Chinese

Features & facilities
Child friendly
 - High chairs
Disabled facilities
Non-smoking area
Private functions
Wheelchair access

Aroma is designed along clean modern lines and offers open plan dining from a central buffet carousel.

This is an 'eat as much as you like for a fixed price' buffet restaurant where you can dine on oriental cuisine in a stylish yet informal atmosphere at an affordable price. The food is always delicious, well cooked and well presented. Wines and drinks are reasonably priced.

It also includes a Tepanyaki section where you can select your own ingredients for the Tepanyaki chef to cook to your liking whilst you wait.

Opened in 1997, it is part of a chain of six restaurants in the home counties. Other restaurants are in Basildon, London W12, Wood Green, Luton and Northampton.

There is no need to book but the restaurant is often busy at peak times.

aroma

REDEMPTION
SIGNATURE

10% Discount
Monday to Thursday only
See terms & conditions on page 7. Expiry date: 31 December 2004

Tring

Tring is a classic market town with a stunningly well-preserved Victorian town centre nestling in beautiful open countryside on all sides. To the east is the National Trust land of the Ashridge Estate; to the south lies Tring Park where the Rothschild family came to live in the 1870s and to the north east Ivinghoe Beacon marks the start of the Ridgeway National Trail.

The Grand Union Canal feeds into the Tring Reservoirs at nearby Marstone and Wilstone and the area has become an important nature reserve, all of which makes Tring an excellent base from which to explore the countryside.

The Rothschilds left the town with an invaluable legacy in the shape of many of the town centre's buildings and, most notably perhaps, at the Walter Rothschild Zoological Museum, which is now part of the Natural History Museum.

Although it is agreeably compact, the town offers a surprising abundance of shops ranging from antiques to bookshops and specialist food stores and restaurants catering for every palate and pocket from traditional English afternoon teas to Indian and Italian cuisine. Every Friday the town's bustling atmosphere gets a boost from the lively outdoor market. A farmer's market on a fortnightly basis offers a tempting array of country delicacies.

*Information kindly provided by
the Dacorum Information Centre*

Forno Vivo

(Italian)   (Average Price: £20.00)

Tring (Map Ref: **164** B5)

The Old Post Office
69 High Street
Tring HP23 4AB
Tel: 01442 890005
Fax: 01442 824506
info@fornovivo.com
www.fornovivo.com

The food is simple, well priced and authentic

Opening hours

M-F   10.00am - 10.30pm
Sat   10.00am - 10.30pm
Sun   12.00noon - 10.00pm

Food served

M-F   12.00-3.00 6.00-10.30
Sat   12.00noon - 10.30pm
Sun   12.00noon - 10.00pm

Food style
Italian

Features & facilities
Child friendly
- High chairs
- Children's menu
Disabled facilities
Garden/Outside eating area
Non-smoking area
Private functions
Special diets catered for
Vegetarian dishes
Wheelchair access
Wines - extensive selection

Forno Vivo's simple but effective philosophy is to use the skills of their chefs, superb ingredients and a real Italian wood burning oven to produce fantastic food at a reasonable price.

The restaurant is set in the old Post Office and cleverly combines historical heritage with modern stylish decor. The restaurant is spacious with comfortable seating and high ceilings. The wood burning oven in the corner creates a focal point and the aroma of freshly cooked pizzas wafts gently around the restaurant. At the back there is now a new conservatory and a garden for a true continental dining experience.

Forno Vivo's signature dish is wonderful handmade real Neapolitan pizza cooked in the wood burning oven. But there is more than just pizza. There are plenty of other great Italian dishes including a range of starters, pastas, salads, panini and sweets. Sunday is very popular, when one of the restaurant's trademark dishes, Agnello alla Romana – a shoulder of lamb slow roasted, Italian style – is served.

Four charity nights and occasional theme evenings are held during the year.

A comprehensive range of Italian wines are offered along with a range of Italian liqueurs. Coffee and pastries are available throughout the day.

The Jubraj Tandoori

Tring (Map Ref: **164** B5)   (Indian) (Average Price: £15.00)

53a High Street
Tring HP23 5AG
Tel: 01442 825368

*A traditional Indian
restaurant serving a wide
range of dishes*

Opening hours

M-F	12.30-2.15	6.00-11.45
Sat	12.30-2.15	6.00-11.45
Sun	12.30-2.15	6.00-11.45

Food style
Indian

Features & facilities
Air conditioned
Child friendly
Garden/Outside eating area
Non-smoking area
Private functions
Special diets catered for
Vegetarian dishes

The Jubraj Tandoori is an established restaurant and has built a loyal clientele who return regularly for the quality food and service.

This is a large restaurant with an eclectic mix of colours and styles. The stone water feature, bright red arches, hanging plants, wood carvings and fish tank all help to create a lively atmosphere. There are also a few tables outside for you to relax and enjoy a drink before your meal.

The Indian cuisine is predominently from the Bangladeshi region although there are influences from other regions as well. Vegetarians are well catered for with a variety of dishes to choose from.

The restaurant is open seven days a week for lunch and dinner. It is fully licensed and serves a full range of wine and traditional Indian beers. Booking is recommended at weekends and other peak times.

It is conveniently located just off the High Street, next to the main car park, but please note that the car park is sometimes used for the town's market so parking may be restricted.

The Valiant Trooper

(Modern English)   (Average Price: £20.00)   **Aldbury** (Map Ref: **164** B5)

Trooper Road
Aldbury, Nr Tring HP23 5RW
Tel: 01442 851203

*The Valiant Trooper
boasts an extensive
pedigree of accolades*

Opening hours
M-F 11.30 amd - 11.00pm
Sat 11.30 amd - 11.00pm
Sun 12.00noon - 10.30pm

Food served
Mon 12.00-2.00
Tu-F 12.00-2.00 6.30-9.15
Sat 12.00-2.30 6.30-9.15
Sun 12.00-2.30

Food style
Modern English

Features & facilities
Child friendly
- Children's menu
- High chairs
Garden/Outside eating area
Non-smoking area
Real ales
Special diets catered for
Vegetarian dishes
Weddings /private functions
Wines - extensive selection

Aldbury is a pretty rural village near Tring on the Hertfordshire and Buckinghamshire borders and a popular area for walkers and cyclists.

The Valiant Trooper is a family run establishment, owned by Tim and Helen O'Gorman. It has been an ale house for over 200 years and was originally called The Royal Oak. Rumour has it that the Duke of Wellington once met his troops here to discuss tactics – hence its current name. The building is unpretentious and set a short distance from the village green with a large car park at one side.

The main bar area is a typical English pub with low ceilings and exposed beams. The restaurant is housed in an old, renovated stable and is light and spacious.

The varied menu is displayed on a blackboard and changes daily. There is a variety of English, French and international dishes. Examples include brocolli and stilton soup; creamy tarragon chicken breast or beef fillet strips in a brandy and mushroom sauce. There is always a good selection of vegetarian dishes. The menu is complemented by a comprehensive wine list and real ales.

The Valiant Trooper boasts an extensive pedigree of accolades and is recommended by the Which Pub Guide, the AA and Egon Ronay.

Ware

including Great Amwell

Ware Highlights

• Scott's Grotto

• The Gazebos on the River Lea

• Ware Priory

For more information on the town and surrounding villages contact:

Tourist Information Point
Ware Museum
High Street, Ware

Summer opening hours:
Tues, Thurs, Sat 11.00am-5.00pm
Sun 2.00pm-5.00pm

Winter opening hours:
Tues, Thurs, Sat 11.00am-4.00pm
Sun 2.00pm-4.00pm

Bank holidays: 2.00pm - 5.00pm

Information kindly supplied by the Tourist Information Point, Ware Museum

No introduction to Ware would be complete without a mention of 'The Great Bed of Ware', which, as its name suggests, is simply a great big bed. Thought to have been made in the 16th century as an advertising gimmick for one of the many local inns, it now resides in the Victoria and Albert Museum and was mentioned in Shakespeare's Twelfth Night.

In fact the town is also mentioned by Samuel Pepys and in Chaucer's Canterbury Tales because it is on the pilgrimage route to the shrine of the Virgin Mary at Walsingham, which explains the proliferation of inns and pubs in the town – a tradition that's very much alive today.

Among many other intriguing sites, including the gazebos that line the River Lea, Scott's Grotto is probably Ware's strangest. Built in the late 18th century by the Quaker poet John Scott, it's a classic 'folly' and a fascinating one at that! Its six underground chambers, linked by passageways, are lined with myriad flints, fossils and seashells and if you look hard enough you can find the word 'frog' spelled out in shells somewhere! Don't forget your your torch.

It is no surprise that Ware's designated a centre of 'outstanding archaeological and historical interest' but there are plenty of other attractions that are bang up to date, such as the big band and rock concerts in the Priory grounds, the annual Dickensian Evening and carol concert each Christmas time and a diversity of restaurants and nightlife that are the envy of far larger towns.

With a direct rail link to London's Liverpool Street station and the A10 just a mile away, Ware is as well-connected with the capital as it was in the days when the River Lea was its lifeblood.

Zodiac Restaurant, Hanbury Manor

(International) (Average Price: £50.00)   **Ware** (Map Ref: **163** G4)

Hanbury Manor
Hotel and Country Club
Ware SG12 0SD
Tel: 01920 487722
Fax: 01920 487692
www.hanbury-manor.com

*Fine dining at its
very best*

Opening hours

Tu-Th 12.30 - 2.00
7.30 - 9.30
Fri   12.30 - 2.00
7.00 - 9.30
Sat   7.00 - 9.30
Sun 12.30 - 2.00

Food style
Continental - a modern
twist on the best English
and French cuisine

Features & facilities
Non-smoking restaurant
Special diets catered for
Vegetarian dishes
Wines - extensive selection

Zodiac is the award-winning fine dining restaurant at Hanbury Manor. The stunning Jacobean House set amidst 200 acres of glorious countryside provides the perfect backdrop for dining out in style with its rich-coloured buildings, beautiful gardens and magnificent interior.

The restaurant's stunning decor overlooks the magnificent golf course and its lake, providing the perfect backdrop to a truly gastronomic experience. From the imaginative menu with its modern twist on French cuisine, to the carefully selected fine wines, the exemplary service and attention to detail, this exquisite 2AA - rosette restaurant is a must for all food lovers. Table d'hôte and à la carte menus are available.

Popular dishes include the spiced breast of quail with green peppercorn and chilli dressing and the tournedos of black gold beef with seared foie gras and winter truffles. For a true gastronomic feast the 'Taste of Hanbury' menu is designed to lead the palate through a host of different flavours and textures.

Enjoy a range of classic and modern drinks prior to dining in the Cocktail Bar. Afterwards relax with a coffee, a fine cognac, or a game of chess in the wood-panelled Oak Hall or Library.

Oakes Grill, Hanbury Manor

Ware (Map Ref: **163** G4) (International) (Average Price: £32.00)

Hanbury Manor
Hotel and Country Club
Ware SG12 0SD
Tel: 01920 487722
Fax: 01920 487692
www.hanbury-manor.com

A contemporary, light and airy restaurant with a stunning terrace for al fresco dining

Opening hours
M-F 7.00am - 10.00pm
Sat 7.00am - 10.00pm
Sun 7.00am - 10.00pm

Food style
International

Features & facilities
Child friendly
 - High chairs
 - Children's menu
Non-smoking restaurant
Outside eating area
Special diets catered for
Sun terrace
Vegetarian dishes
Wheelchair access
Wines - extensive selection

Oakes Grill is the second award-winning restaurant at Hanbury Manor. The stunning Jacobean House set amidst 200 acres of glorious countryside provides the perfect backdrop for dining out in style with its rich-coloured buildings, beautiful gardens and magnificent interior.

Relax in the contemporary, light and airy restaurant which enjoys views over the 18th green of the hotel's championship golf course. Oakes Grill provides dining to suit all palates throughout the day. Each dish is prepared using the best ingredients and with a two course menu priced from £25.00 and three-courses from £32.00, it also provides real value for money. Current favourite dishes include the spicy prawn and shallot parcel with chilli jam and the crispy confit of duck leg with white bean and chorizo cassoulet. Also on offer is the 'all day dining' menu which is perfect for those with a smaller appetite.

Open seven days a week, Oakes Grill also offers a Sunday Jazz and Champagne Brunch and other special dining events throughout the year.

For those occasions that demand a more casual and informal atmosphere, Vardon's provides the answer. This ground floor lounge bar is open all day from 7.30am serving a range of light snacks.

Jacoby's

Churchgate House
15 West Street
Ware SG12 9EE
Tel: 01920 469181
Fax: 01920 469182

*Classical food with a
modern twist*

Opening hours
Mon 6.00pm-11.00pm
Tu-Fr 11.00am-11.00pm
Sat 11.00am-11.00pm
Sun Closed

Food served
Mon 7.00pm-9.30pm
Tu-Fr 12.00noon-2.30pm
     7.00pm-9.30pm
Sat 12.00noon-2.30pm
     7.00pm-9.30pm
Sun Closed

Food style
A contemporary mix of
British, French and oriental
cuisines

Features & facilities
Child friendly
 - High chairs
Garden/outside eating area
Non-smoking area
Special diets catered for
Weddings/Private functions
Wines - extensive selection

Jacoby's opened in April 2002 in the historic
Churchgate House in the centre of Ware. The
building dates back to the 16th century and is
Ware's second oldest building. The restaurant
is based on two floors with the bar and
smoking section on the ground floor and an
entirely non-smoking area on the first floor.

The menu changes regularly taking inspiration
from home and around the world. Dishes are
designed to suit all tastes, appetites and
pockets and adjusted to include seasonal
produce and trends. Fresh produce is at the
heart of the cooking which has been described
as classical in its preparation with a modern
twist.

At full capacity the restaurant accommodates
up to 100 diners. Friday and Saturday are the
busiest nights of the week and you are advised
to book 2-3 weeks in advance.

Jacoby's offers an extensive wine list with
wines from around the world to complement
every dish. Wines range in price from £11.50
to £50.00 a bottle.

The ambience is casual yet sophisticated and
is matched by the surroundings. This historic
building has been tastefully modernised to
include exposed beams, a feature staircase
and a glass atrium.

Le Rendez Vous Restaurant

Ware (Map Ref: **166** G5)　　(Modern European)　(Average Price: £25.00)

64 High Street
Ware SG12 9DA
Tel:　01920 461021
Fax: 01920 423351

*Only the finest
ingredients are used
offering an excellent
balance of flavours*

Opening hours

M-F　12.00-3.00　7.00-Late
Sat　12.00-3.00　7.00-Late
Sun　12.00-4.00

Food style
Modern European

Features & facilities
Child friendly
Garden/Outside eating area
Non-smoking area
Special diets catered for
Vegetarian dishes
Weddings/Private functions
Wheelchair access
Wines - extensive selection

You will receive a warm welcome from proprietors Jorge and Lesley. The atmosphere is always relaxed and friendly.

The building dates back to the 16th century with charming oak beams which add to the ambience. Alternatively, weather permitting, try the pretty enclosed terrace garden for an al fresco dining experience.

Lunches are a set menu of two or three courses. A full à la carte menu is served in the evenings and at around £25 a head offers excellent value for money. It also includes a range of vegetarian options. On Sundays a traditional Sunday lunch is served until late afternoon - a family day when children are welcome.

The cuisine is modern European, using only the finest ingredients and offering a balance of flavours. An extensive wine list with over 40 different wines from around the world complements Jorg's superb dishes.

Every Wednesday night is 'Spanish Night', with a selection of hot and cold tapas - the seafood paella is always a winner.

REDEMPTION
SIGNATURE

**10% Discount
Monday to Friday**

See terms & conditions on page 7. Expiry date: 31 December 2004

Three Lakes Restaurant & Function Room

(Contemporary English) (Average Price: £30.00)   **Ware** (Map Ref: **166** G5)

Westmill Farm
Ware SG12 0ES
Tel: 01920 468668
Fax: 01920 469290
threelakesrestaurant@yahoo.co.uk
www.threelakes.co.uk

*Spectacular views, great
food and friendly service*

Opening hours

Mon Closed
Tu-Sa 12.00noon - 11.00pm
Sun 11.00am - 6.00pm

Food served

Tu-Sa 12.00-4.00 7.00-11.00
Sun 12.00-4.00

Food style

Contemporary English

Features & facilities

Child friendly
- Baby changing facilities
- High chairs
Disabled facilities
Garden/Outside eating area
Non-smoking restaurant
Private functions
Special diets catered for
Vegetarian dishes
Wheelchair access
Wines - extensive selection

Golf course (par 3)
Three fishing lakes

This new, family run restaurant has already gained a reputation for exquisite food, breath-taking views and friendly service.

The Three Lakes' evening menu boasts many scrumptious choices including best end of lamb with garlic and rosemary crusting served with redcurrant jus. There are also a range of mouth-watering starters and not-to-be-missed homemade desserts. It's the perfect setting for a romantic evening for two or dinner with friends.

At lunchtime there is a 'quick and casual' menu which is ideal for business lunches. Guests can also enjoy a drink in the garden.

There is also a separate, fully licensed function room which can accommodate between 10 to 70 guests - ideal for any occasion.

The Vigus family have farmed at Westmill Farm for over 60 years. Their redevelopment also includes the three Rib Valley fishing lakes, a par 3 golf course, remote control car racing and Top Pots Garden Centre.

The Three Lakes Restaurant and Function Room at Westmill Farm is half a mile from the A10 on the A602 towards Stevenage.

three
lakes
restaurant
& function room

REDEMPTION
SIGNATURE

10% off lunch (Food only)
Tuesday - Saturday

See terms & conditions on page 7. Expiry date: 31 December 2004

131

George IV

Great Amwell (Map Ref: **166** G5)   (English/British)   (Average Price: £17.00)

Cautherly Lane
Great Amwell, Ware SG12 9SW
Tel: 01920 870039

*The menu is generally
British but is influenced
by tastes from around the
world*

Opening hours

M-F	11.30-3.00	6.00-11.00
Sat	11.30-3.00	6.30-11.00
Sun	12.00-3.00	7.00-10.30

Food served

M-F	11.30-2.00	6.00-9.00
Sat	11.30-2.00	6.30-9.00
Sun	12.00-2.00	7.00-9.00

Food style

English/British but with influences from around the world

Features & facilities

Child friendly
 - High chairs
Garden/Outside eating area
Non-smoking area
Private functions
Real ales
Special diets catered for
Vegetarian dishes
Wines - extensive selection

People travel from all over the county to visit this popular pub and restaurant.

Set in the small village of Great Amwell the attractive restaurant has a vaulted ceiling and an airy open bar. The patio area in front of the pub is popular for barbeques in the summer.

The separate restaurant at the back of the pub is usually only open in the evenings and at weekends but the bar area is very comfortable for lunch or, if the weather is good, you can sit outside and enjoy the country air.

The menu is generally British but is influenced by tastes from around the world. There is also a daily specials board for you to choose from.

On the first Tuesday of each month a 'theme evening' is held based on different types of cuisine. Recent evenings have included Indian, French and seafood.

There is a well stocked bar which includes over 12 malt whiskies, a wine list that spans both old and new world countries and a selection of well kept real ales.

Booking is advisable at peak times. The George IV also caters for small, private parties and functions.

Watford

including Aldenham

Watford Highlights

- Watford Football Club

- Cassiobury Park/ The Grand Union Canal/River Gade

- The Harlequin Shopping Centre

- St Mary's church (c1230)

All the great invaders of Britain seem to have set foot in Watford - including the Saxons, Vikings and Romans – and all are associated with a different theory about how Watford acquired its name. The Saxon version is that the word wath meant hunting and a ford, of course, is a suitable place to cross a river ...

Whilst the Roman version is that the original Watford settlement was the one nearest Watling Street, the main Roman road and was also an excellent fording point – hence Wat-Ford.

By the Middle Ages, the village had becoming a thriving market town packed with tanners, millers, bakers, brewers and butchers and, increasingly, thousands of Londoners escaping the capital's overcrowding and epidemics. Growth doubled with the advent of the Grand Union Canal and by the end of the First World War, Watford attracted the printing, brewing and light engineering industries. Mothercare, for example, began life in Watford, and Benskins, the brewing giant, has long been based in the town.

Today, the town is a truly cosmopolitan place with a thriving nightlife, ranging from restaurants, pubs and the Jongleurs Comedy Club, which features all the nation's top comics, to the Destiny and Area nightclubs for night owls and hard core clubbers. The elegant Edwardian Palace theatre stages around nine shows a year, while the Watford Coliseum hosts pop, rock and classical concerts.

But since it is so close to London and so urban in style, it's easy to forget that the beauty of Watford is that it sits at the heart of the Green Belt and has endless open space with parks, cycle tracks and of course the Canal right next door.

Il Carnevale - that's Amore

Watford (Map Ref: **165** D7)

(Italian)　(Average Price: £25.00)

195 St Albans Road
Watford WD24 5BH
Tel:　01923 247750

The restaurant buzzes at weekends with friendly banter in a relaxed atmosphere

Opening hours

M-F　12.00-2.30　6.30-11.00
Sat　Closed lunchtime
　　　6.30-11.00
Sun　Closed

Food style
Italian - specialising in fish and seafood

Features & facilities
Child friendly
- High chairs
Vegetarian dishes
Wheelchair access
Wines - extensive selection

Il Carnevale – that's Amore, is a restaurant with a real love for quality Italian cooking as its name implies.

Set in the busy St Albans Road it has been a family-run restaurant for over 32 years but under new management since December 2002.

Owner Luigi brings a vibrance to the establishment and offers you a warm welcome as you enter his restaurant - you'll soon feel like one of the family! The restaurant buzzes at weekends with friendly banter in a relaxed atmosphere.

Fish and seafood are the restaurant's speciality with the fish dish pepata one of the most popular choices from the varied menu.

The restaurant is light and bright and pleasantly decorated with plants and flowers.

Booking is advisable from Thursday to Saturday.

REDEMPTION
SIGNATURE

Free bottle of house wine
for tables of 2 or more Mon-Thurs

See terms & conditions on page 7.　Expiry date: 31 December 2004

The Bowl Chinese Restaurant

(Chinese) (Average Price: £10.00)

Watford (Map Ref: 165 D7)

318A-320 St Albans Road
Watford WD24 6PQ
Tel: 01923 250460
Fax: 01923 250460

*The ultimate Chinese
eating experience - eat
as much as you like from
the buffet*

Opening hours

M-Th	12.00-2.30	6.00-11.00
Fri	12.00-2.30	6.00-11.30
Sat	12.00-2.30	6.00-11.30
Sun	12.00-5.00	6.00-11.00

Food style
Chinese & South Asia

Features & facilities
Child friendly
- High chairs
Disabled facilities
Private functions
Vegetarian dishes
Wheelchair access

The owners of The Bowl Chinese Restaurant describe it as "the ultimate eating experience" and they're not far off the mark. On offer is good quality traditional Chinese food served from a smart and stylish hot buffet table.

The open plan restaurant is light and relaxed with 150 spacious seats. Fully air conditioned it offers an elegant setting with a friendly atmosphere.

With a range of six starters, two soups and seven main courses at lunchtime for just £5.00 it is superb value for money. In the evenings the range extends to eight or ten starters plus everyone's favourite - crispy aromatic duck. Again, at just £9.00 per person midweek and £10.00 on Friday or Saturday it's excellent value and don't forget - it's eat as much as you like.

Parking can be tricky but there are car parks nearby in Lockspring Road and The Harebreaks.

REDEMPTION
SIGNATURE

Order one jug of cocktail and
get one free - Monday-Thursday

See terms & conditions on page 7. Expiry date: 31 December 2004

The Round Bush Public House

Aldenham (Map Ref: **165** D7)

(English/British) (Average Price: £14.00)

Roundbush Lane
Aldenham, Watford WD25 8BG
Tel: 01923 855532

*A traditional British pub
serving generous
portions of good, home
cooked pub food*

Opening hours

M-F 12.00noon - 11.30pm
Sat 12.00noon - 11.30pm
Sun 12.00noon - 10.30pm

Food served

M-Tu 12.00-3.00
W-Sa 12.00-3.00 6.00-8.30
Sun 12.00-4.00

Food style
English/British

Features & facilities
Child friendly
 - Children's menu
Disabled facilities
Garden/Outside eating area
Non-smoking area
Private functions
Real ales
Vegetarian dishes
Wheelchair access
Wines - good selection

The Round Bush is a great value traditional British pub - good food, friendly banter and a well stocked bar.

The building dates back to the 1830s and the current owners have been here for nearly four years. The restaurant is non-smoking and has recently been refurbished.

Children are welcome and there is a safe garden with small play area and a special 'Monty's Menu' for them to choose from. And the garden even has an outside serving area to save you venturing inside.

The lunchtime menu includes a wide range of filled jacket potatoes, baguettes, bloomers and 'Roundbush Burgers'. The evening menu is more extensive and the portions are generous - try the 14 oz T-bone succulent prime steak, cooked to your liking. Everything is cooked to order and most of the meat comes from a local supplier.

The bar is well stocked and has a good selection of wines and four real ales to choose from.

REDEMPTION
SIGNATURE

One child eats free from children's menu with 4 adults, Mon-Thurs.

See terms & conditions on page 7. Expiry date: 31 December 2004

Chiquito

Garston, Watford (Map Ref: **165** D6)

Woodside Leisure Park
Kingsway, Garston
Watford WD25 7JZ
Tel: 01923 682321
www.chiquitowatford.co.uk

*A Mexican theme
restaurant with a great
atmosphere*

Opening hours

M-F	12.00noon - 11.00pm
Sat	12.00noon - 11.00pm
Sun	12.00noon - 10.30pm

Food style
Mexican

Features & facilities
Child friendly
- High chairs
- Children's menu
Disabled facilities
Non-smoking area
Private functions
Vegetarian dishes
Wheelchair access
Wines - extensive selection

If you fancy a fun night out or a lively lunch then "come to Chiquito!" says manager Lorna Bailey-Amrouche. "It's Mexican for fun, for fantastic food, for an amazing atmosphere and for a good time - guaranteed".

Chiquito offers authentic Mexican cuisine, which is freshly prepared and cooked on the premises, at a reasonable price. With its unique Mexican interior and lively Mexican and Latin American music, Chiquito really is a great night out.

Try one of the famous sizzling fajita platters – Acapulco chicken or maple glazed salmon are just a couple of the favourite platters. Chiquito offers a varied selection of reasonably priced wines but, to really get the evening going, try one of the famous Margaritas or cocktails.

The restaurant is open 7 days a week so it's an ideal venue for a quick lunch, a bite after work or a lively party with friends and family.

REDEMPTION
SIGNATURE

10% Discount
Sunday to Thursday inclusive

See terms & conditions on page 7. Expiry date: 31 December 2004

Welwyn and Welwyn Garden City

Welwyn Highlights

- Welwyn Roman baths

- Stanborough Park, Lakes, Watersports Centre and Nature Reserve

- Mill Green Museum and Mill

- Shaw's Corner, Ayot St Lawrence

For further information about this area contact:

Welwyn Garden City Library
The Campus
Welwyn Garden City
AL8 6AJ
Tel: 01438 737333

Information kindly supplied by
Welwyn Garden City Library

Welwyn Garden City was one of the 'new towns' created after the First World War to reduce overpopulation and poor housing in the big cities - a social experiment on a massive scale.

Fortunately for its inhabitants, the garden city concept based on the original thinking of Ebenezer Howard has proved to be a resounding success. It is largely thanks to that great reformer that the overriding impression as you enter this now mature neo-Georgian city is one of space, greenery and a laid-back atmosphere that belies the hustle and bustle at the city's heart, where the elegantly expansive John Lewis department store and the new Howard Centre draw shoppers from miles around.

But the new has not ousted the old and there is a wealth of local landmarks and sites of historical and cultural interest. The Welwyn Roman Baths are a good example. Ingeniously preserved in a vault under the A1M at Welwyn Village, this third century bathing suite provides a fascinating insight on the way Romans lived on a day-to-day basis.

At the Mill Green Museum you can see the fully restored and operational 18th century watermill in action and you can even buy the authentic organic wholemeal stone-ground flour it produces.

As you'd expect of a planned city, the sport, entertainment and leisure amenities are excellent: Stanborough Lakes provides sailing, windsurfing and fishing; sports and fitness facilities are available at the Gosling Sports Complex and all kinds of music, drama and cinema events are held at the vibrant Campus West Centre.

The White Horse

30 Mill Lane
Welwyn AL6 9ET
Tel: 01438 714366
www.thewhitehorse-welwyn.co.uk

*Excellent food - freshly
prepared on the
premises*

Opening hours

M-F	12.00-3.00	5.30-11.00
Sat	12.00-4.00	5.30-11.00
Sun	12.00-4.00	6.30-10.30

Food served

M-Tu	12.00-2.00	
W-F	12.00-2.00	7.00-9.00
Sat	12.00-2.00	7.00-9.00
Sun	Two sittings 12.00 & 2.00	

Food style
English/British plus a range
of Italian pizzas

Features & facilities
Garden/Outside eating area
Parking
Private functions
Real ales
Wines - extensive selection

A charming 17th century coaching inn set in Old Welwyn with many nearby attractions including the Roman Baths, Hatfield House and Knebworth House.

The food is excellent and freshly prepared on the premises. Carnivores are well catered for, with wonderful T-bone, rump or sirloin steaks, or the locally produced Braughing sausages.

For a lighter meal, try one of the authentic wood smoked pizza - at £5.45 for a 9" or £8.45 for a 12" they are excellent value for money. Or you can create your own, with traditional toppings such as sausage, chicken, peppers, chillies, mushrooms, tuna, olives and many more, all freshly prepared by their chef, Tallisimo.

A comprehensive range of beers, wines, champagne, fine malts and whiskies are also on offer.

The gardens are delightful, with a paved terrace and well kept lawns and a range of stylish steel tables and chairs. Summer barbeques are always popular, with outdoor heaters to keep you warm. In the winter, relax inside by the cosy log fire.

Business seminars, weddings, private functions and golf societies are all well catered for and bed and breakfast accommodation is also available.

The Stable Door

Welwyn (Map Ref: 162 F4) (English/British) (Average Price: £18.00)

12 High Street
Welwyn AL6 9EQ
Tel: 01438 715200
www.thestabledoor-welwyn.co.uk

*Good food, fine wines
and attentive service
make eating here an
enjoyable and
flavoursome experience*

Opening hours
Mon Closed
Tu-F 12.00-3.00 6.30-11.00
Sat 12.00-3.00 6.30-11.00
Sun Closed

Food served
Mon Closed
Tu-F 12.00-2.00 6.30-9.30
Sat 12.00-2.00 6.30-9.30
Sun Closed

Food style
English/British - specialising
in fish and seafood

Features & facilities
Non-smoking area
Private functions
Real ales
Vegetarian dishes
Wine and Champage -
  extensive selection

This award winning 17th century bistro,
with its wooden floors and appealing decor,
has an unpretentious, warm and welcoming
atmosphere.

Owners Joan and Chris and family, apply a
simple yet appealing philosophy to create
excellent food and outstanding value for
money in a relaxed and homely atmosphere.

The Stable Door's speciality is fish and
seafood. Freshness is guaranted and the
menu changes daily. The cooking is simple to
enhance the flavours of the food.

Large succulent prawns, finest smoked
salmon, lemon sole, turbot, halibut, sea bass
are just some examples of the extensive
range of fish and seafood on offer.
Homemade casseroles, pastas and vegetarian
dishes are also served to help to make The
Stable Door one of the most popular venues
in the area.

Good food, fine wines and attentive service
make eating here an enjoyable and
flavoursome experience.

Please note that the restaurant upstairs is
exclusively non-smoking.

Tewin Bury Pie Restaurant

(English/British) (Average Price: £20.00) **Nr Welwyn** (Map Ref: 165 F5)

Photography by Andrew Buckle & Picture This

Tewin Bury Farm Hotel
Nr Welwyn AL6 0JB
Tel: 01438 841490 / 717793
Fax: 01438 840440
Email: hotel@tewinbury.co.uk
www.tewinbury.co.uk

A privately owned 17th century farmhouse set in the idyllic Hertfordshire countryside. Modern British food with an international twist

Opening hours

M-F   8.00am - 9.30pm (last orders)
Sat   8.00am - 9.30pm (last orders)
Sun   8.00am - 9.30pm (last orders)

Food served

M-F   12.00-2.30pm, 7.00-9.30pm
Sat   12.00-2.30pm, 7.00-9.30pm
Sun   12.30-1.30pm, 3.30-9.30pm
Booking advisable

Food style

English/British

Features & facilities

Child friendly
 - High chairs
 - Children's menu
Garden/Outside eating area
Limousine, Taxi & Minibus
  Service
Non-smoking area
Special diets catered for
Vegetarian dishes
Weddings/Private functions
Wheelchair access
Wines - extensive selection

The Williams family has farmed in Hertfordshire for over sixty years but some time ago decided to turn the farmhouse and its surrounding buildings into a 29 bedroom country house hotel.

'The Pie' as its devotees now know it, was transformed from one of the original, derelict farm buildings into a 60-seater restaurant that can bring a real sense of occasion to your afternoon or evening out.

The menus have flair and imagination and the dishes are freshly prepared using the finest local produce.

Tewin Bury's relaxed and informal atmosphere and its commitment to excellence, combine to ensure your function or meal will be a success and your stay enjoyable.

To make your visit to Tewin Bury Farm a completely carefree treat, spoil yourself by booking one of the limousines, taxis or minibuses from Tewin Bury Carriage Company (tel: 01438 717771).

TEWIN BURY FARM HOTEL

141

The Plume of Feathers

Tewin (Map Ref: 165 F5)   (English/British)   (Average Price: £20.00)

57 Upper Green
Tewin, Welwyn AL6 0LX
Tel: 01438 717265
Fax: 01438 712596
8646@greeneking.co.uk

*Winner of the Best Food
Pub of the Year 2003 for
the Greene King Pub
Company*

Opening hours
M-F 12.00noon - 11.00pm
Sat 12.00noon - 11.00pm
Sun 12.00noon - 10.30pm

Food served
M-F 12.00-2.30 6.30-9.00
Sat 12.00-2.30 6.30-9.00
Sun 12.00noon - 8.00pm
Booking is advisable at all times.

Food style
English/British

Features & facilities
Child friendly
 - High chairs
Disabled facilities
Garden/Outside eating area
Non-smoking area
Private functions
Real ales
Special diets catered for
Vegetarian dishes
Wheelchair access
Wines - extensive selection

Built in 1596, this historic inn, which is a former hunting lodge of Elizabeth I and later the haunt of highwaymen, now boasts several ghosts including a 'lady in grey'. These days a warm welcome awaits everyone.

The building and gardens are impressive and as you enter you get that feeling of comfort that only a few places can give. The staff are quick to ascertain whether you wish your visit to be a formal or more informal occasion. The interesting layout means you can enjoy a quiet corner table, or be a part of the atmospheric hub.

Head chef, Jason Fretwell, prides himself on the freshly prepared and cooked on the premises menu he offers, for both lunch and dinner, and also the many daily-changing dishes.

Special features include the Tapas Bar serving authentic tapas from noon until close every day – just right when a meal would be too much and a bag of crisps won't quite hit the spot.

Enjoy al fresco dining all summer long in the magnificent gardens with wonderful views over rolling hills and woodlands. There are two cosy log fires to keep you warm in the winter.

A great selection of wines from around the world is on offer and the range of cask ales have been 'cask marque accredited' so you know you are being served a perfect pint.

Auberge du Lac

Brocket Hall,
Welwyn AL8 7XG
Tel: 01707 368888
www.brocket-hall.co.uk

*One of the finest places
to eat in Hertfordshire*

Opening hours

Mon Closed
Tu-Fr 12.00-2.30 7.00-10.00
Sat 12.00-2.30 7.00-10.00
Sun 12.00-2.30 Closed

Food style
International

Features & facilities
Garden/Outside eating area
Special diets catered for
Vegetarian dishes
Weddings/Private functions
Wheelchair access
Wines - extensive selection
Child friendly
 - High chairs

Auberge du Lac is the inspired result of a comprehensive and elegant design and refurbishment programme. Set in the magnificent parkland of Brocket Hall, Auberge du Lac upholds the finest culinary standards and further enhances Brocket Hall's reputation for excellence.

A former Hunting Lodge dating back to 1760, the building sits proudly alongside the water's edge in its own peaceful environment, overlooking the splendour of the Estate. It is exquisitely furnished, with panoramic views beyond its own garden setting.

This statement from Directeur des Cuisines, Jean-Christophe Novelli, gives an insight into the culinary delights of his restaurant "Cooking is my great passion. I relish being adventurous and creating innovative modern cuisine based on classical French principles. Each dish on the menu combines texture, a daring blend of flavours and the finest ingredients".

In addition to the A la carte menu there is also a fixed price lunch menu for £28.00 midweek or £35.00 at the weekend.

The wine list is exceptional with wines to suit every taste and pocket.

If you are celebrating a special occasion then Auberge du Lac will provide the perfect venue.

Index – food types

Index - food types

Index – food types

Index - food types/features and facilities

Features and facilities

Child friendly with special children's menu available

Child friendly with high chairs available

Index – features and facilities

Town	Restaurant	Telephone	Page

Child friendly with high chairs available, continued

Index - features and facilities

Town	Restaurant	Telephone	Page
Aldenham, Watford	The Round Bush	01923 855532	136
Garston, Watford	Chiquito Restaurant & Bar	01923 682321	137
Welwyn	Tewin Bury Pie Restaurant	01438 717793	141
Tewin, Welwyn	The Plume Of Feathers	01438 717265	142
Welwyn	Auberge Du LacLac	01707 368888	143

Disabled facilities

Baldock	Old White Horse	01462 893168	10
Barnet	Grittz Restaurant	020 8275 9985	14
Barnet	Spizzico	020 8440 2255	16
Barnet	Emchai	020 8364 9993	18
Barnet	Caffé Uno	0208 441 6112	19
Barnet	The Palace	020 8441 7192	20
Berkhamsted	Caffé Uno	01442 874856	22
Bishops Stortford	Host Restaurant & Bar	01279 657000	25
Spellbrook, Bishop's Stortford	The Three Horseshoes	01279 722849	26
Bishop's Stortford	Caffé Uno	01279 755725	27
Bishop's Stortford	The Lemon Tree	01279 757788	28
Borehamwood	Signor Baffi Restaurant	020 8953 8404	30
Turnford, Broxbourne	Cheshunt Marriott Hotel - Washington Restaurant	01992 451245	33
Broxbourne	The Highland Restaurant	01992 466933	34
Cottered, Buntingford	The Bull	01763 281243	36
Brent Pelham, Buntingford	The Black Horse	01279 777305	38
Bushey	Blue Check	020 8421 8811	41
Bushey	St James	020 8950 2480	42
Croxley Green, Rickmansworth	The Coach & Horses	01923 774457	102
Harpenden	The Bean Tree	01582 460901	46
Harpenden	New Taj Mahal	01582 715280	47
Harpenden	The Old Bell	01582 712484	48
Brookmans Park, Hatfield	Methi Indian Cuisine	01707 662233	53
Brookmans Park, Hatfield	Brookmans Park Hotel - Gobions Restaurant,	01707 653577	54
Hertford	Elbert Wurlings	01992 509153	61
Hertford	The Stone House	01992 553736	63
Stapleford, Hertford	Le Papillon - Woodhall Arms	01992 535123	68
Watton-at-Stone, Hertford	The George & Dragon	01920 830285	70
Little Berkhamsted, Hertford	Five Horseshoes	01707 875055	71
Hitchin	Restaurant Mirage	01462 615019	73
Redcoats Green, Hitchin	Redcoats Farmhouse Hotel & Restaurant	01438 729500	75
Letchworth	Sagar Tandoori Restaurant	01462 675771	85
Much Hadham	The Bull Inn	01279 842668	88
Reed, Royston	The Cabinet	01763 848366	104
St Albans	Sopwell House - Magnolia Restaurant	01727 864477	107
St Albans	Waffle House	01727 853502	109
St Albans	Wagamama	01727 865122	110
St Albans	Cafe Des Amis	01727 853569	112
St Albans	Gastrodome	01727 851941	113
Redbourn, St Albans	The Chequers Inn	01582 792359	115
London Colney, St Albans	The Colney Fox	01727 823698	116
Codicote, Stevenage	The Bell Motel & The Vines Cafe	01438 821600	119
Stevenage	Aroma Oriental Restaurant	01438 352183	121
Datchworth, Knebworth	Coltsfoot Country Retreat	01438 212800	120
Tring	Forno Vivo	01442 890005	123
Ware	Three Lakes Restaurant & Function Rooms	01920 468668	131
Watford	The Bowl Chinese Restaurant	01923 250460	135
Aldenham, Watford	The Round Bush	01923 855532	136
Garston, Watford	Chiquito Restaurant & Bar	01923 682321	137
Tewin, Welwyn	The Plume Of Feathers	01438 717265	142

Index – features and facilities

Index – features and facilities

Special diets

The following restaurants cater for special diets but you are advised to mention your requirements when booking.

Index – features and facilities

Town	Restaurant	Telephone	Page

Special diets, continued

Vegetarian dishes

The following restaurants offer a selection of vegetarian dishes but are not entirely vegetarian restaurants.

Index – features and facilities

Index - features and facilities

Town	Restaurant	Telephone	Page

Index – features and facilities

Wheelchair access

Index - features and facilities

Town	Restaurant	Telephone	Page

Wheelchair access, continued

Index – restaurants and pubs

Index – restaurants and pubs

Index – restaurants and pubs

Index – towns and villages

Maps – pages 161–166
© Collins Bartholomew Ltd 2003
Reproduced by permission of
Harper Collins Publishers at
www.bartholomewmaps.com

Scale

3.2 miles to 1 inch

0	1	2	3	4	5	6 miles

0	2	4	6	8	10 km

2 km to 1 cm

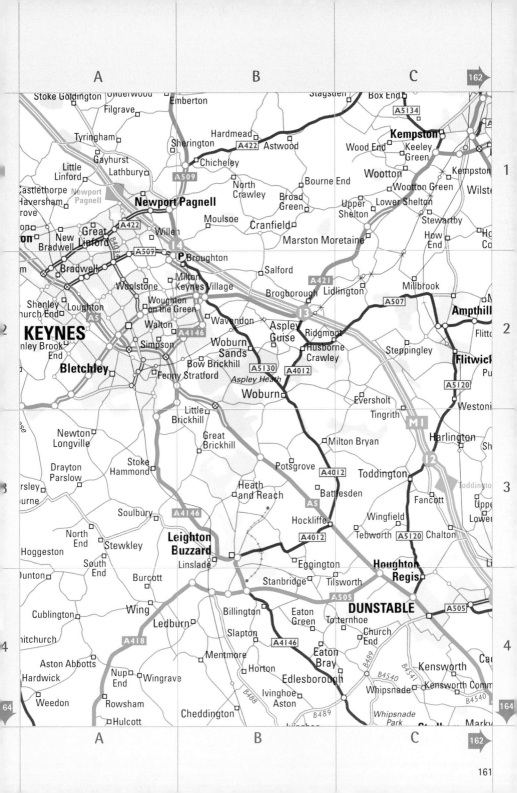

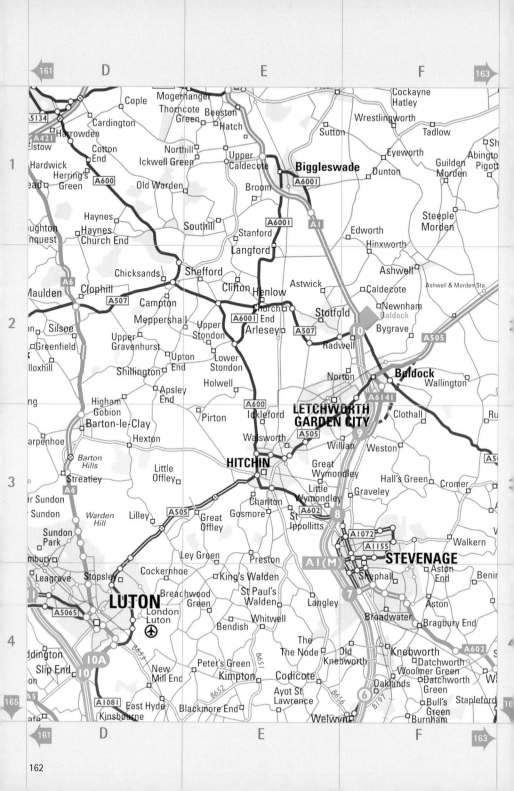

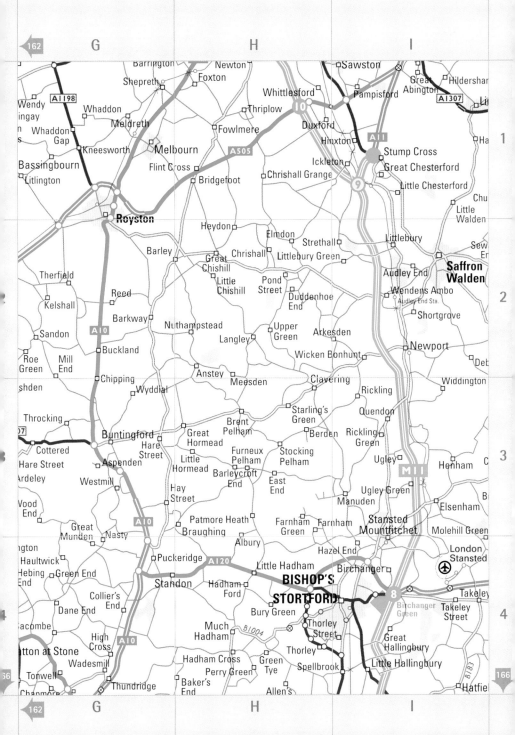

G   H   I

Barrington   Newton   Sawston   Great   Hildersha
Shepreth   Foxton   Pampisford   Abington
Whittlesford

Wendy   A1198   Whaddon   Thriplow   10   Duxford   A1307   Li
ingay   Meldreth
Whaddon   Fowlmere   Hinxton   A11   Ha
Gap   Kneesworth   Melbourn   A505   Ickleton   Stump Cross
Bassingbourn   Flint Cross   Great Chesterford
Litlington   Bridgefoot   Chrishall Grange   9   Little Chesterford
                 Chu
Royston   Heydon   Little
           Elmdon   Strethall   Littlebury   Walden
Barley   Chrishall   Littlebury Green   Sew
Great   En
Therfield   Chishill   Pond   Audley End   Saffron
Little   Street   Walden
Kelshall   Reed   Chishill   Duddenhoe   Wendens Ambo
             End   Audley End Sta.
Sandon   Barkway   Nuthampstead   Shortgrove
Roe   Mill   A10   Langley   Upper   Arkesden
Green   End   Buckland   Green   Newport
shden   Chipping   Anstey   Wicken Bonhunt   Deb
     Wyddial   Meesden   Clavering   Widdington
Throcking   Rickling
07   Brent   Starling's   Quendon
Cottered   Buntingford   Great   Pelham   Green   Berden   Rickling
Hare   Hormead   Green
Hare Street   Street   Little   Furneux   Stocking   Ugley   Henham
Ardeley   Aspenden   Hormead   Pelham   Pelham   M11
Westmill   Barleycroft   East   C
Vood   Hay   End   End   Ugley Green
End   Street   A10   Manuden   Elsenham
Great   Patmore Heath   Farnham   Farnham   Stansted   Molehill Green
ngton   Munden   Nasty   Braughing   Green   Mountfitchet
Haultwick   Albury   London
Hebing   Green End   Puckeridge   Hazel End   Stansted
End   A120   Little Hadham   Birchanger
acombe   Standon   Hadham   BISHOP'S   8   Takeley
    Collier's   Ford   STORTFORD   Birchanger   Takeley
Dane End   End   Bury Green   Green   Street
atton at Stone   High   A10   Much   Thorley   Great
    Cross   Hadham   B1004   Street   Hallingbury
Wadesmill   Thorley   Little Hallingbury
Tonwell   Hadham Cross   Green   Spellbrook
Chanmore   Thundridge   Baker's   Perry Green   Tye   Hatfie
          End   Allen's

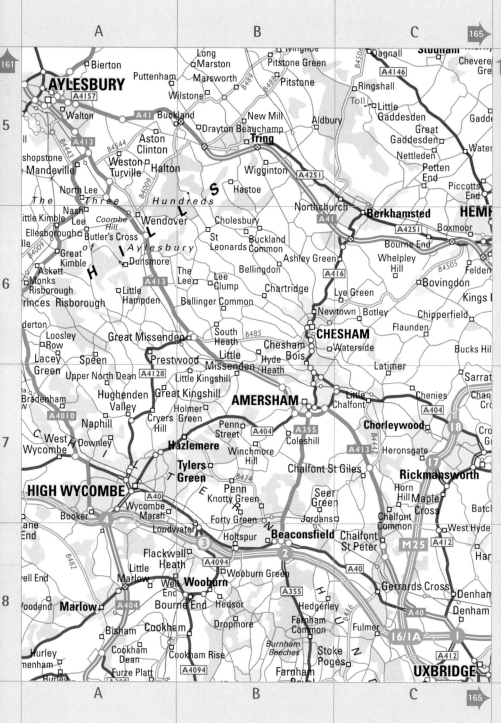

Bierton
Long Marston
Pitstone Green
Dagnall
Studham
Chevere
Gre

AYLESBURY
Puttenham
Marsworth
Pitstone
Ringshall
A4146
Gadd

Walton
Buckland
New Mill
Aldbury
Toll
Little Gaddesden
Great Gaddesden
Water

Aston Clinton
Drayton Beauchamp
Tring
Nettleden
Potten End

Weston Turville
Halton
Wigginton
A4251
Northchurch
Piccotts End

shopstone Mandeville
North Lee
Hastoe
Berkhamsted
HEMP

The Three Hundreds
Boxmoor

little Kimble
Nash Lee
Wendover
Cholesbury
St Leonards
Buckland Common
Bourne End
Whelpley Hill
Felden

Ellesborough
Coombe Hill
Butler's Cross
Ashley Green
B4505

Great Kimble
of Aylesbury
Dunsmore
Bellingdon
A416
Bovingdon
Kings

Askett
Monks Risborough
The Lee
Lee Clump
Chartridge
Lye Green
Chipperfield

rinces Risborough
Little Hampden
Ballinger Common
Newtown Botley
Flaunden

derton
Loosley Row
Great Missenden
South Heath
B485
CHESHAM
Waterside
Bucks Hil

Lacey Green
Spey
Prestwood
Little Missenden
Chesham Bois
Latimer
Sarrat

Upper North Dean
A4128
Little Kingshill
Hyde Heath
Chenies
Chan
Cro

Bradenham
A4010
Hughenden Valley
Great Kingshill
Holmer Green
AMERSHAM
Little Chalfont
A404

Naphill
Cryers Hill
Penn Street
A404
A355
Coleshill
Chorleywood
18

West Wycombe
Downley
Hazlemere
Winchmore Hill
A413
Heronsgate
17

Tylers Green
Chalfont St Giles
Rickmansworth

HIGH WYCOMBE
A40
Penn
B474
Seer Green
Horn Hill
Maple Cross
Batcl

Booker
Wycombe Marsh
Knotty Green
Jordans
Chalfont Common
West Hyde

Loudwater
Holtspur
Beaconsfield
Chalfont St Peter
M25
A412
Har

Flackwell Heath
A4094
Wooburn Green
A40
Gerrards Cross
Denhan

Little Marlow
Well End
Wooburn
A355
Hedgerley
Denham

Marlow
A404
Bourne End
Hedsor
Farnham Common
Fulmer
16/IA
A40
1

Bisham
Cookham
Dropmore
Burnham Beeches
Stoke Poges
A412
UXBRIDGE

Hurley
Cookham Dean
Cookham Rise
A4094
Farnham

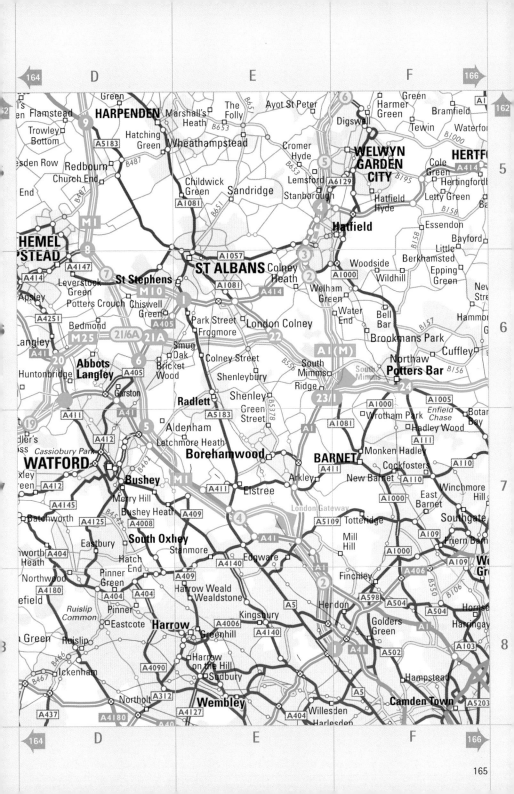

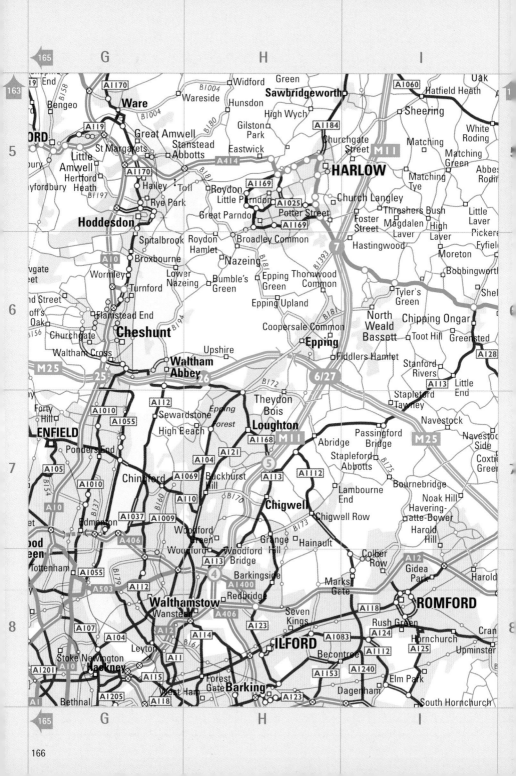